MARINE PILOT

John Foot

Ian Henry Publications

ISBN 0 86025 922 6

Some of the material in this book has previously appeared in
The Illustrated Diary of a Thames Pilot

Published by
Ian Henry Publications, Ltd.,
20 Park Drive. Romford, Essex RM1 4LH
and printed by
Gomer Press, Llandysul, Ceredigion SA44 4QL

To pilots past and present, and the launch crews to whom they entrust their lives

Sunset and evening star,
And one clear call for me!
Any may there be no moaning of the bar,
When I put out to sea...

Tennyson: Crossing the bar

Moyana inward bound at the Needles   Summer 1951

Chapter One

First Steps

Perhaps, at some stage, it is every boy's dream to go to sea, but having failed the Dartmouth entrance exams at the tender age of thirteen, my ambitions received a setback. Enthusiasm remained however, and I was drawn like a magnet to the docks at Littlehampton. Watching the bustle of the small Sussex port, the arrival and departure of small coasters, and the movements of countless fishing and pleasure craft.

I befriended the harbourmaster, who assured me that it would be pointless making the sea my career unless I made a 'dummy run' at least to ensure that I wouldn't be seasick! He invited me to make a trip on the dredger that was to be delivered the following day to Newport, Isle of Wight, some 30 miles away. I jumped at the chance, and stood with him in the small wheelhouse, watching carefully as he gave me my first lesson in seamanship, conning the vessel through the narrow entrance of the River Arun, where the pier heads stretched far out to sea. Commander Diaper spun the wheel to starboard, and steadied the vessel on course for the island, a blue smudge on the horizon. He explained the compass and the lubber line, and invited me to take the wheel. He watched briefly at my assumed nonchalance. I wonder if he noticed my white knuckles gripping the spokes! "Just keep her steady, I'm going below for a moment," he said.

I could hardly believe it. My first sea voyage, alone on the bridge, and steering too! I stared fascinated at the compass card. It all seemed too easy for words. As long as the lubber line remained steady against the course I was steering, there was no problem. I relaxed and felt like shouting aloud!

Dredger

I looked again at the compass. I had not moved the wheel, yet already the ship's head was drifting away from the W.S.W. I turned the wheel tentatively and gradually, to my horror, the lubber line swung further from the course. The more I turned the wheel, the faster the dredger swung. I looked up, panicstricken. The sands of Littlehampton lay dead ahead. My first and last sea voyage? The harbourmaster was back in the wheelhouse, grinning hugely as he brought the dredger back on course. "You aren't the first one," he said, "don't forget, it's not the compass moving, but the lubber line or ship's head. I don't expect you'll make that mistake again."

Not long afterwards the opportunity arose for me to spend a month on the Metcalfe coaster *John M*, for which my parents were charged a princely £5. I joined the ship in Shoreham during the discharge of a coal cargo. The air was black with coal dust, and everywhere covered with it. But this didn't deter me, I couldn't wait to get started. Perhaps the Captain would allow me to steer. On second thoughts, perhaps he should not! I was introduced to the crew as I joined them in the small mess room for supper. I remember volunteering to assist in the hold cleaning in the morning, but the Chief Engineer quickly dissuaded me. "You'll be black from head to foot, and ruin all your clothes." From that moment I was careful to pick and choose my jobs.

My first visit to the bridge was after dark and the Mate pointed out the red side light of a vessel crossing. This was my first introduction to the 'Rules of the Road' as we turned to starboard under the other's stern. I steered occasionally too, but made no mention of my previous steering experiences! I also managed to be seasick, but only once after yet another large meal soon after departure from Plymouth and into a moderate swell. My job in port was to go ashore and buy the papers and any odd stores the steward required. We plodded up and down the coast at a very sedate 8 knots loading and discharging our cargoes of coal. I remember Aberdeen - beautiful in the early morning with the sunrise reflected in the windows of the town. And Amble, only a very small port but within easy reach of magnificent Alnwick Castle by bus and well worth the visit. And so to my final port, and my first experience of the busy Thames, to Stepney. Little did I realise it then, but that was where my future lay, a Trinity House pilot who would make many hundreds of trips up and down that famous river.

My enthusiasm for the sea gathered momentum even though there were no seafarers in my family. Despite my careers master at school trying to divert my interest, I enrolled as a cadet at the School of Navigation, Warsash, in the autumn of 1950. The school is situated on the bank of the River Hamble overlooking the Solent and the oil refinery of Fawley on the opposite shore. Set in beautiful grounds, with sports fields, tennis courts, with the magnificent training ketch *Moyana* moored at the end of the pier, together with many other craft at our disposal. I was going to enjoy this.

But I had reckoned without Captain Wakeford! The school's Director had only one year to fashion a raw recruit into something resembling an officer cadet in the Merchant Navy. A first term cadet had no time to enjoy himself; this was make or break time for the forty youngsters from all parts of the world who joined each term. If they could handle that first term, they would be able to manage anything the future held.

It was a harsh regime under the strictest discipline. Orders were obeyed without hesitation, and at the double. Juniors were the lowest of the low, at the beck and call of the 'intermediates' who in turn were wary of the seniors in there final term. Whilst everyone stood in awe of the Chief Cadet Captain and his various lieutenants. During the first weeks of indoctrination I wondered if I was making a sensible choice, for the junior's lot was not a happy one! Rising at 5.30, an hour before 'reveille', polishing boots and brass work, etc. Then the morning run, cold shower, and back to cleaning the cabins, burnishing the wooden decks, and making the 'drapes' which entailed folding both sets of bedclothes from the upper bunk, sheets outside with not a crease. Then followed the daily inspection from the Duty Officer who marked each cabin accordingly. The bugle ran our lives, but what a relief to be called to breakfast with what seemed a full day's work already done! A relief also when the day's lessons began, as we were introduced, half asleep, to the mysteries of Seamanship and Navigation.

On one occasion in the early days as I doubled through the grounds from one duty to another, I passed two gentlemen in civvies. I had not seen either before, but when I had passed, there came a great roar from behind, "Cadet!" I doubled back, sensing trouble, and saluted. But it was too late. "Report yourself to your Cadet Captain, who will give you 2 hours drill." I had failed to recognise Captain Stewart, second in command of the school. Just like the lubber line on that compass, I didn't make that mistake again, and thereafter saluted everyone on sight!

'Drill' was carried out in full battledress with rifle and of course, at the double. For lesser crimes, 'Overtime' was the usual punishment, and meted out in generous quantities. One visiting Sunday, my parents arrived and watched in astonishment as I doubled past in boiler suit pushing a wheelbarrow!

The cadet in charge of our cabin of six, was a Burmese called Bhattacharjee. He was in his mid-twenties and had already served in the Burmese navy. A strict disciplinarian, he was determined that our cabin would turn out the 'Best Guard' of the week. This 24-hour duty involved colour duties at morning parade, ceremonials at 'Sunset', and rounds during the night. Unfortunately, despite Bhattacharjee's strict training, events did not go according to plan on our first full parade. The two raw recruits, a Greek cadet and myself, had been given the least responsible task of bending on the Red Ensign to the halyards. Two steps forward, two back, eyes front all the time, strict tempo.

"Parade, shun. Guard, present arms!" The bugle sounded, and that was our cue. With slow measured pulls of the halyard, the flag reached the top of the yardarm as the last strains of the bugle died away.

"Lower that flag immediately," screamed the Parade Officer, his face purple with rage. And no wonder, the flag was upside down! If I was learning from my mistakes, I was learning fast, and doing extra drill the next day.

'Rounds' for the Duty Guard would entail a specific job, such as, "0200- Proceed to boat house, check all secure, then proceed to *Moyana* and South Hill [radar pinnace], check all secure." A Duty Guard came badly unstuck one night. Instructions had been left to ensure that 'Salterns', the director's beautiful home overlooking the Hamble, was secure. Captain Wakeford had left a lounge window slightly ajar, and on the sill were six beers and a note to the Guard Commander. In the morning neither the window nor the beers had been touched. The result was two hours drill times 6, and they didn't achieve Best Guard that week either!

Royal Inspection. Warsash Cadets at HMS *Excellent*, Whale Island

Judo was another discipline to which we were encouraged to pay close attention. Mr Noice, the European middle-weight champion, had little time to lick his raw recruits into shape. And heaven help anyone not paying full attention. "Bloggs," he would shout to a victim who thought he was well hidden at the back of the circle, "You obviously know this throw. Come and demonstrate for us all." We knew what was coming. If his throw was not perfect, Noice would demonstrate again and again as the unfortunate, bruised cadet rose gingerly from the mat! In the years to follow that training was to stand many of us in good stead in the less desirable ports of the world.

During his year, each cadet spent 2 weeks training on the 100 ton *Moyana*, either on a cruise of a week or so, or day cruises or simply on overnight anchor watches. The first requirements were to learn all the ropes and rigging, blocks and tackles, and to be able to identify these in the dark. *Moyana* was Captain Stewart's pride and joy, and woe betide any sloppy seamanship or failure to instantly carry out his orders.

On one memorable occasion leaving her Hamble moorings under sail, *Moyana* threaded her way down river, dwarfing all around her as she made her majestic departure. My cabin mate, that same Greek cadet, was at the wheel for the first time. Captain Stewart stood at his side giving him precise helm orders, then as the foresails partially obstructed his view, he walked to the foredeck and continued the 'con' from there. All went well until he called out an unaccustomed order. "Come up, cadet, come up." (*i.e.* Nearer the wind). The order was repeated, the cadet froze, his English was limited, and he had been told to come up. He ran to the foredeck, the wheel spinning unheeded, and saluted the Captain smartly. For a moment Captain Stewart was at a loss for words, but then, calm and assured as always, he instructed the cadet to return to his duty at the wheel. It was on the same cruise that the same cadet, working high in the rigging of the mainmast, managed to drop his marline spike which embedded itself firmly in the teak deck - at Captain Stewart's feet! Earlier that cadet had received 2 hours overtime for slack seamanship. Now, in addition, he was to receive 2 hours drill.

In the summer of 1956 *Moyana* hit the headlines with a front page picture in the *Daily Telegraph*. This was the year of the first International Sail Training Ship race, from Torbay to Lisbon. Amid great celebration Captain Stewart was presented with the trophy by Marshal Francisco Lopes, President of Portugal. But alas, within a fortnight *Moyana* was once again front page news. During her return trip she encountered a raging storm in the Channel, began taking water and left Captain Stewart little option but to abandon ship. Fortunately the 9000-ton cargo ship *Clan Maclean* (Captain Cater) was standing by and in heavy seas drew alongside the stricken vessel. Perfect judgment and a good lee enabled the entire crew to scramble up the cargo nets and lifelines that had been rigged over the ship's side. *Moyana* sank soon after despite efforts to tow her. The fifteen young cadets received heroes' welcomes when they were landed at Fowey, and soon after there followed a victory parade through the streets of Southampton.

Despite the rigours of those first weeks at Warsash, this was more than compensated in the final term, and then the prospect of really going to sea. Interviews were conducted with various shipping companies. There were plenty of vacancies for cadets in the 1950s. We were spoilt for choice, and yet which was the best? New Zealand Shipping, Blue Funnel, Royal Mail, Clan Line, Bibby, P & O, the famous names rolled off the tongue. I bought myself a shipping manual in which all the cadets' rates of pay were quoted. Silver Line offered the highest, rising to £15 per month in the fourth year. I went for an interview, was accepted and, after a long summer holiday, received instructions to join *Silverguava* in Middlesbrough, starting at a salary of £7 per month.

Chapter Two

Apprenticeship

The rain beat ceaselessly against the carriage window as I gazed out at the gathering gloom of the November evening. Gradually the train slowed as we approached the outskirts of Middlesbrough. I stood up, studying my reflection in the mirror, adjusted my tie again, checked the buttons of my reefer jacket and set my cap squarely above the anxious face. I gave myself a nervous smile. Surely there were worse things in life than joining one's first ship, and setting off upon a voyage of perhaps two years! Perhaps, like my father, I should have joined the bank after all.

There were not many people on the platform, but at the ticket barrier an important looking man in uniform and peaked cap. "You must be the new apprentice. Follow me." We drove through the town towards the docks. Shops and offices gradually gave way to warehouses, cranes, derricks, superstructures and funnels. We passed through the gates of the drydock, rounded a corner, and there was my first ship

My immediate impression of the *Silverguava* was her immense size; she seemed to dwarf everything around her, even though she was only a modest 5000 tons. Another lasting memory was the floodlights of both ship and dry-dock highlighting the freshly painted grey hull, white superstructure, and the blue and white funnel. To me she appeared beautiful even though she was already twenty-five years old.

A Malay seaman took the two suitcases from my hands as I stood looking up the steep gangway. "Follow me," instructed my guide once more. We walked along the decks, then mounted several stairways. He knocked on a door on the lower bridge. "Good evening, Captain Duncan. I've brought your new apprentice."

My first ship: *Silverguava* 5000 tons gross. Built 1927

There were three other apprentices onboard *Silverguava* and we shared a cabin on the main deck. It was strange to be a new boy again, and yet again on the first rung of the ladder. But this was the 'real thing' I felt, and the real beginning of my career at sea.

That year at Warsash was to stand me in good stead throughout, not least on that first morning when the Chief Mate ordered us to climb through the manhole of a fresh water tank to scale, clean and lime wash. And so at last my first voyage began, with the dry-dock flooded, and tugs easing *Silverguava* out into the river on passage for Antwerp. I was put on the 8-12 Watch with the 3rd Mate, and my job that first night at sea, was to keep a sharp look-out from the wing of the bridge. A cold, lonely vigil, and I felt envious of the Malay quartermaster steering the ship, sharing the comfort of the wheelhouse with the OOW.

Suddenly, in the middle of the North Sea, the steady thumping of the engines ceased and the lights went out. "Hoist the N.U.C (Not Under Command) lights," bawled Mr Bright, the 3rd Mate. Panic! I had no idea where they were let alone how to hoist them. I rushed about looking as busy as possible (something I had soon learned at Warsash!), and eventually, behind the bridge, in a large locker covered with lifeboat stores, I found the two large brass oil lanterns.

"Matches?"

"Down below in my cabin."

"Oil?"

"Get some from the bosun's store."

I managed to fight my way up the vertical ladder to the monkey island. I found a halyard, bent on the lanterns and hauled away. It was as well that I did not stand directly beneath, for no sooner had the halyard taken the weight, the rope parted and the lanterns crashed to the deck. It was impossible to re-light them on the exposed monkey island, so back down to the wheelhouse and up again, this time to hoist the lights on separate halyards. I am ashamed to admit the job took an hour, by which time full power had been restored. But I was learning fast; the next day the halyards were renewed, the lamps primed and matches to hand, though *Siverguava* never broke down again.

The rendezvous for picking up the pilot for ships bound Antwerp, is the A1 Buoy some twenty-five miles from the river Scheldte entrance at Flushing. So far from land, it seemed strange to me that we couldn't proceed further without assistance. It was here that my first seeds of interest in pilotage were sown. I imagined that it might be fun manœuvring ships in restricted waters and if one day the opportunity arose, who knows?

Antwerp proved to be a disappointing first port. Cold, dirty and with many hours on standby during the long river passage and lock systems. So it was with relief, after further loading in London, that we set course down Channel to warmer climes on the other side of the world.... Australia.

* * *

The routine of a long voyage was soon established. There were 50 souls onboard comprising British officers, Malay seamen, Indian firemen, Goanese stewards, half a dozen passengers and of course not forgetting four apprentices. The Bay of Biscay, Mediterranean, Suez, Red Sea, all magical names to me, but only from the pages of an atlas. Then into the Indian Ocean leaving Cape Guardafui and the Horn of Africa behind us, and into the gentle N.E. Monsoon to temper the increasing warmth.

For some these were lazy, idyllic days, sunbathing or swimming in the makeshift canvas pool, but we were kept busy working on deck side by side with the Malays, learning how to overhaul cargo gear, grease wires, chipping and painting, cleaning brasswork, checking lifeboat equipment, and the numerous other routine jobs required of a seaman. In addition we kept watches on the bridge learning from the mates the mysteries of celestial navigation, in exchange for endless cups of tea and sandwiches through the long night hours. But unlike the chill North Sea, keeping lookout on those balmy nights under a myriad of stars, clad only in a pair of shorts, was sheer bliss, and one's imagination ran riot. It felt almost as if we were suspended in space.

After more than a month at sea, it came as an anti-climax to have to anchor off Adelaide for a fortnight awaiting a berth. But the time passed pleasantly enough with lifeboat picnics to the distant beach where we received the unwelcome attention of large blue crabs. Perhaps their territory had never been invaded before, for they were aggressive creatures and no sooner had we jumped from the boat into the crystal clear water, they would move rapidly into the attack. But we had the last laugh. Wearing suitable footwear, and armed with sticks to which were attached lengths of rag, the crabs would get snarled up, hoisted out of the water and into a waiting sack. It was a foolproof method and we enjoyed crab salads for many weeks afterwards. Twelve years later and in the same month, while serving in P & O’s *Himalaya*, I was to visit that beach again with a boat load of friends armed with sticks and rags, assuring them of a massive haul. We did not see a single crab!

We were to spend three weeks discharging our general cargo, so even busy apprentices found time to sample the delights of beautiful Adelaide. One social event was a dance organized by the Missions to Seamen’s padre. We felt very gauche after two months aboard ship, sat facing several middle-aged women across the floor. But eventually I summoned up courage and asked one lady to dance. She wasted little time in remarking that I didn’t dance very well. I didn’t like to tell her that I would have preferred the chair I had been taught to dance with at navigation school!

The padre proved to have considerable influence over the Chief Mate, for we apprentices were to spend a week painting the roof of the pavilion at the Missions to Seamen sports ground, using ship's paint! In return we enjoyed the hospitality of the vicarage, with hazy recollections of his two pretty daughters.

Our voyage continued across the Pacific to the Hawaiian Islands: a short stop for bunkers and mail, and then on to the west coast of the U.S.A. The sprawling city of Los Angeles offered little attraction, but nearby Hollywood was worth a visit. Then on to beautiful San Francisco: the Golden Gate, Alcatraz, Fisherman's Wharf... so much to see.

All too soon our cargo was loaded and it was time to cross another ocean. From one continent to another, a month apart and half way round the world, entombed as we were in our 'time capsule', a small ship upon a mighty sea. From America to India, and Calcutta one hundred miles up the Hooghly river. From one culture to another, completely different. The people, the heat and humidity, the smells, the abject poverty, the beggars, the sacred cows walking the streets, the burning ghats, all these ingredients providing unforgettable memories of a country one can never tire of learning about. And to lie in a hammock slung on the boat-deck, watching the dawn break through the mists of the river, with fleets of fishermen casting their nets from narrow boats as they drifted by on the silent tide, provide memories which will remain forever etched in my memory.

My first voyage ended after eleven months when *Silverguava* at last returned to Europe. But our arrival in Rotterdam was tempered with sad news. Our trusty ship, after twenty-six years of sterling service with Silver Line, was to be sold for scrap. She had served us well.

* * *

By tramping standards in those days, a voyage of only one year was considered to be on the short side. On the other hand, for an apprentice to have four months leave was most unusual, and I already had itchy feet when I received my marching orders to join the brand new *Silverburn* in Hartlepool. Compared with the old *Silverguava*, this latest addition to the fleet looked immaculate and we apprentices were of the impression, soon mistaken, that we would have a soft job! Of the same size as my previous ship, *Silverburn* was built for the carriage of homogeneous cargoes such as grain, coal, ore etc, with longitudinal bulkheads running through the centre-line of the ship. Ideal for tramping but with a very modest speed of ten knots.

The accommodation for the four apprentices was a vast improvement on the main deck where our cabin had been vulnerable in heavy weather. Now we shared a roomy cabin on the lower bridge deck, with a small study/lounge adjoining. The only disadvantage was the close proximity of the Mates along the alleyway, with the Captain and Chief Mate above. I still found myself the junior apprentice, though not quite a greenhorn anymore, and I was delighted that Captain Duncan had also been appointed to the ship. John Duncan had served with distinction during the war, not least when in command of *Silverlarch*.

Smiling faces: author front right

His ship had just completed discharge of munitions, explosives and rolling stock in Sumatra when Japanese forces reached there and it soon became apparent that the invaders would overrun the island. The naval authorities asked Captain Duncan to return alongside to reload tanks and army transports. By then there were no pilots and the channel buoyage had been removed. Undeterred John Duncan completed the reloading and a human cargo of 2300 women and children landing them safely in Java. Unhappily these refugees had but a short reprieve for Java was soon to fall into Japanese hands

After sea trials, and the departure of shore personnel, *Silverburn* commenced her maiden voyage in ballast, bound for the West Indies. One apprentice was placed on each watch, whilst the fourth was day worker. The daylight hours were, as usual, spent working on deck with the Malay seamen. There was plenty do on a new ship, stowing away large quantities of stores, paints, ropes and wires, checking equipment in the lifeboats, cargo gear to be tested for although everything was new, it was now our responsibility to make sure it all worked upon arrival at our first port of loading. The night watches were spent on the bridge under the supervision of the Mates. Through the English Channel and the Western approaches that extra pair of eyes peering into the reduced visibility was invaluable, but as we set course S.W across the Atlantic towards the Tropics, there was time enough to tackle the mysteries of navigation. How a sextant was used to establish the ship's position, whether by altitude of a heavenly body, the altitude of a distant headland or lighthouse, or even the horizontal angle between charted marks. We learned that an angle from a sextant produced a position circle upon which the observer must be situated, and that where two position circles bisected each other must establish the observer’s position. Easy enough now, but magic then. Looking up into the heavens, identifying the major stars from the constellations in which they belonged, and learning to plot our position from them with the aid of tables, sextant and chronometer.

We plotted our slow progress down across the Atlantic. It took a powerful magnifying glass to identify our destination, Great Inagua, among the numerous islands of the West Indies, situated north of the Windward Passage which separates the islands of Cuba and Haiti. We dropped anchor off the port of Matthewtown, and awaited our turn to load our first cargo, salt for the American west coast. In addition to the two lifeboats, we were equipped with a 15 foot jolly boat and outboard motor. This proved much handier and easy to launch for picnic parties to the magnificent beaches with no living soul within miles. Both shark and barracuda were observed from deck, but they didn't disturb our enjoyment of the surf.

And so fully loaded and earning her first freight, *Silverburn* headed for the Panama Canal and on to her port of discharge, Tacoma. And then on hire again, northwards to Vancouver Island. We were to spend an idyllic month there loading timber. The scenery was magnificent, and some of the ports consisting of nothing more than a few weatherboard houses and small wooden jetties. New Westminster, Victoria, Chemainus, Cowicham Bay and Port Alberni.

In port one early morning a fellow apprentice and I were on deck overhauling cargo gear, when a shout came from above. There on his deck stood Captain Duncan, a towel round his ample waist. "Foot, lower the jolly boat. We're going fishing." We returned in time for breakfast with two large salmon taken with spinning rods. There were black looks from the Chief Mate whose apprentices had been playing truant!

It was a pleasant surprise to return to England after a mere four months away. Part discharge in London and Avonmouth, and then down to the Mediterranean for completion in Gibraltar and Malta. Empty again, but not for long. There was plenty of work for tramp ships, and La Goulette in nearby Tunisia had a cargo of iron ore on offer. What an ideal opportunity to visit the ancient ruins of Carthage, whose violent history dates back to the Phoenicians in the 9th century B.C., the Roman Empire, and its final devastation by Arabs at the end of the 7th century. We hired a horse drawn carriage and explored the ruins of temples and amphi-theatres. Carthage does not attract many tourists even now. During our visit it was deserted, and as our horse ambled through the ruins it was as if we were suspended in another two thousand year time warp.

One of the advantages of serving in a tramp company operating relatively small ships was the opportunities to visit those parts of the world off the beaten track. Such an example was the Philippines which consists of thousands of islands, many uninhabited. The main product for export is dried coconut or copra, and *Silverburn* was much in demand as she threaded her way from village to village. We loaded at a leisurely pace, sometimes moored to a rickety jetty, or anchored in a small inlet with our stern ropes secured to trees. At each port the laden barges drew alongside, and the ship swarmed with Filipino stevedores. A time to lock and secure everything for their eyes were everywhere and pilfering their second nature. There was always a guitarist among them, and at every meal break the gangs would sit in a circle accompanying the beautiful haunting chords. To listen to such music under a mantle of stars, with the lights of the nearby village reflected in the still water will remain another of my lasting memories. And in the same breath too, could one ever forget the beautiful girls? They hypnotized us, especially we young apprentices, and when, after a month of gathering in our cargo, it was time to say farewell, there was a lump in the throat and a tear in the eye.

Upon our return to Europe, a surveyor boarded the ship in Rotterdam and condemned the cargo. Apparently, despite the full ventilation and open hatches during the passage home, some of the copra, perhaps damp when loaded, had rotted and contaminated the remainder.

After the bliss of the Philippines, fate spun the other side of the coin with a visit to the Baltic in mid-winter to load coal. Our destination was Gdansk, so cold that an ice-breaker had to clear a path for us, and even then it required ‘full ahead’ on the engine-room telegraph to crunch our way through the ice bordering the jetty. At the bows we lowered our mooring ropes to men standing on the ice, and they walked them to the bollards ashore.

Gdansk was altogether a miserable experience, made doubly so by all the water pipes, hot and cold, freezing up while all about us the air was thick with the dust of our cargo. A thick, black mantle enveloped every open space, and not a drop of water. But there was one small compensation, the steam pipes to the winches had drain-cocks, and so with a bucket of ice and a length of hose we managed a wash of sorts.

The Polish people had little to smile about under the communist regime so soon after the war, but the mention of Winston Churchill would soften their gray, pinched faces. The port was under strict security, and heavily armed guards patrolled the jetties at the bow, stern and gangways of each ship. Each guard stood twelve hours duty, marching back and forth in the bitter cold, heavy greatcoat with rifle slung on top. The Malay crew had caused some ill feeling laughing at the guards' discomfort. Then, in the early hours of one morning, a guard took one step too many - through the ice he fell, straight to the bottom. By morning the ship was very much under suspicion, and it took much diplomacy from Captain Duncan to calm the increasing numbers of high ranking officials.

The customs guards at the dock gates were on constant lookout for the smuggling out of cigarettes. The allowance was one packet of twenty, and one of our engineers was strenuously searched by a burly female official who found an additional packet hidden away. Despite the language barrier she made it abundantly clear that he would suffer imprisonment - unless... He was instructed to wait until the end of her shift, whereupon he was escorted to her flat, and allowed to leave, a free man, in the morning!

At last the coal was loaded, the ship prized away from her berth by two large tugs and the ice-breaker. Our new ship, the pride and joy of the Silver Line, covered from main-truck to lowest deck with black grime, and all the water pipes frozen. It was not until we cleared Ushant, three days later, that the ice melted and we were able to begin the big clean up. But at least we were bound for South America, the River Plate and the warm sun again. After discharge we loaded grain at a small port 200 miles up river, Villa Constitucion, and headed east across the South Atlantic bound South Africa.

* * *

As far as we apprentices were concerned South Africa was the most hospitable country in the world. At each of the major ports, Capetown, Port Elizabeth, East London and Durban, we were treated like long lost relations, fêted with trips ashore and car drives into the outback. In Durban, our agent, an enthusiastic equestrian, invited two officers for an afternoon's riding. The 3rd Mate volunteered, but no-one else, so being the junior I was instructed to make up the numbers. I had childhood memories of a leading rein at walking pace on a very small pony, but if this meant an afternoon off, I'd try anything. Haylett Regenas was a charming man, and he and his friend did their best to put us at our ease during the drive into the hills above Durban. By now alas, my bravado about being a little rusty after a couple of years at sea had dissipated considerably and I enquired whether they had any small ponies available.

I have little recollection of the stables and the beautiful scenery, for I was staring awestruck at the four horses together with their grooms which awaited our arrival. By now I was assuring everyone that I hadn't been on a horse for years, certainly not one that big, and never above a trot. Even at that eleventh hour I could not bring myself to admit to the pony and the leading rein. I thought with longing of all the work I was missing back on dear old *Silverburn*, cleaning brass, oiling wires, chipping, painting... anything.

By the time the groom had assisted my swing into the saddle, I felt somewhat giddy and the ground a long way off, nor was I reassured by 3rd Mate Ralph Pomphrey's sickly face as he fought to control his mount. At first a slow walk to get the feel, and to learn from our hosts upright in the saddle, reins held loosely, knees firm on the flanks. Soon we were trotting through forest with monkeys chattering above us, then laughing as I brought up the rear.

I couldn't seem to synchronize with my mount. I bounced up and down on his back, and tried to grip the reins and his neck at the same time. The two experts had long since disappeared ahead, and Ralph was drawing away at a canter. Soon he was out of sight as well. I suggested to my horse that we might try slowing down, but communication between us had long since broken down, and it was his intention to catch up with his mates - fast.

I clung hard to his neck, and a full gallop we came into a clearing where Ralph lay sprawled on the ground, with his horse grazing peacefully further on. Luckily my mount pulled up, and the two of them had a good laugh as I slid off and hobbled over to my stricken mate. Torn shirts and trousers and bruises were our lasting memories of Durban.

Heavy weather round the Cape

In Cape Town soon afterwards I was to celebrate my twenty-first birthday. Friends ashore had baked me a cake, so had the ship's cook, and the party was in full swing when I was reminded that the 'Old Man' wasn't present. In truth we apprentices stood in awe of the recently appointed Captain Metcalfe, and I had presumed that he wouldn't want to know about the party. How wrong I was! I staggered up to his deck, the worse for drink and knocked on his door. Despite the late hour he was still working at his desk. I had to lean up against it to stay upright. Yes, he had known about the party. I should have sought permission to hold it, and apprentices were not allowed to drink alcohol. I apologized. He declined with thanks my tardy invitation, wished me a happy birthday, and told me to enjoy the rest of the evening. I became drunk for the first time that night - but I always recall Captain Metcalfe as a kindly, fair man.

I was soon to knock on the Captain's door again. The ship had orders for Venice, and having a Swiss girl friend at the time I sought permission for local leave during the four days we expected to be there. He must have shaken his head at such an unusual request from a junior apprentice, but he nodded instead, and we stayed at the Rialto Hotel on the edge of the Grand Canal.

The end of my apprenticeship was in sight, and thoughts of preparing to study for my 2nd Mate's examination. I had kept up a postal correspondence course, and had sat the annual Board of Trade exams at sea. But like my horse riding, I was a little rusty. It was time to return to the School of Navigation, Warsash.

Chapter Three

Joining the P & O

The return to Warsash was a reunion of old friends. Many of us had been cadets together there four years earlier. We spent many an hour sharing the experiences gathered from the far corners of the globe. The conclusions were that some had had a miserable existence, whilst the more fortunate would not have exchanged places with anyone. Some shipping companies had used their cadets as cheap labour with no encouragement, but others had pushed them ahead, and occasionally awarded promotion to Acting 3rd Mate in the third or fourth year of apprenticeship. The East Asiatic Company had been the envy of us all. In Calcutta we had watched in open-mouthed astonishment, in our dirty boiler suits, as one of their ships held a dance on their boat deck. Coloured lights, cadets in smart white uniforms, pretty nurses from a nearby hospital, the soft lilt of a tango across the water. I'd felt we were missing out somewhere.

But Silver Line too had been a good employer. We had been given a thorough grounding, and the company had taken a keen interest in the Captains' reports that were in turn forwarded to parents. The voyages had taken me round the world twice, to little-known places still off the beaten track. But with these voyages lasting a year or more, I wondered whether that might prove too long when the time came to settle down. Several companies offered regular trips of three or four months with leave in between. Perhaps I should consider a change. With the ink hardly dry on my new 2nd Mate's Certificate, I joined the P & O. My first weeks were spent 'dock staffing' during the turn-round of the '*Straths*'' at Tilbury. The *Strathmore, Strathnaver* and *Stratheden* were passenger ships on the Australian run. White hull and superstructure topped with a yellow funnel, these elegant ships were equally popular with passengers and crew alike. It felt very strange in my smart new uniform with the thin blue and gold stripe on each shoulder, as I walked the vast decks and magnificent public rooms finding my way around. I recalled with affection the small *Silverburn*. Had I made the right choice?

With several other 4th Officers on dock staff there were few duties. Repair work and cleaning was done by shore contractors (Green and Silley Weir), cargo discharge and loading was done by the P & O cargo super. We assisted such as surveyors with lifeboats, fire extinguishers, watertight doors, etc. The most important requirement seemed to be the location of light switches and, above all, the flag routine. It took six crew to perform the flag ceremony at 08.00 and sunset.

Chusan, Iberia and *Strathmore* in Tilbury Dock, with an Orient liner far left

The 4th Officer on the bridge with the chronometer, the radio officer at the gramophone and loud-speakers and a *khalasie* (Indian seaman) at each of the flags, stem jack, courtesy flag, house flag and Red or Blue ensign. Today that number would equate to half the crew of a fair sized ship.

But soon after midday at Tilbury there was another ritual that was performed without ceremony, and without fail. As the ship repairers, cleaners and dockers knocked off for lunch, this was the cue for the P & O Dock superintendent and his assistant, the cargo super and his assistant, surveyors and such like. They marched up the gangway and into the dock staff cabins. Gin was the order of the day and one soon learned that one's very prospect of promotion might hinge on the number of refills offered to our illustrious guests! With gin at 4/6d a bottle it was a very cheap investment, though we did not offer tonic water as that cost twice as much. Any variation upon gin and water was the addition of angostura bitters that the company supplied free. These sessions were followed by large lunches in the dining saloon. I cannot recall much work being progressed in the afternoons.

After further spells of dock staff duties on cargo ships in King George V and Royal Albert Docks, I received my first sea-going appointment as 4th Officer of *Cannanore,* 7000 tons gross, on the Indian run. Not much bigger than the Silver Line vessels, and very dour in comparison with her black hull and funnel and stone coloured superstructure. There was a crew of 88, composed of European officers and cadets, Goanese stewards, Indian seamen, Pakistani firemen and the customary Chinese carpenter, an international combination that had served the P & O well for more than a 100 years. There was also accommodation for twelve passengers, which, if filled, brought the total to one hundred, and the legal requirement of a doctor!

The thrill of being at sea again was somewhat tempered by the minor role I played on the bridge. It was the P & O custom to place a new 4th Officer on the 4-8 Watch under the supervision of the Chief Officer until he was considered ready to go solo. Down through Biscay, Mediterranean, Suez and the Red Sea.

Then, at last clear of Aden and into the Arabian Sea and with not a ship in sight, and a clear horizon, I was given the nod. It was not unlike the thrill of driving alone for the first time, without the instructor beside me, and the L-plates thrown away. No doubt the Captain cast an anxious eye from his cabin below as I gave all ships an extra wide berth. Memories of my first trip on the Littlehampton dredger came flooding back as I cast a critical eye at the compass and the seacunny standing at the wheel!

Cannanore in floating dock, Rotterdam

After the casual mode of dress tramping round the world as an apprentice in a tramp ship company, somewhat stricter rules applied in the P & O. Even though *Cannanore* was not one of the 'big white ships', uniforms were *de rigueur* at all times, plus caps. The only concession was the 'Red Sea rig' in the evenings in hot weather. White open neck shirts, black trousers and cummerbund, as opposed to the more formal bow tie and monkey jacket in the passenger ships.

It was back to the Hooghly river and Calcutta again, this time in the middle of the stifling, humid wet SW Monsoon. It is a 120 miles run from the pilot station off Sandheads where the river is so wide that one cannot see either shore, but after Diamond Head there are dangerous shallows and the low lying river banks close in on either side. The final bend brought us to Garden Reach and a first glimpse of the sprawling city. We had hoped to berth in the shelter of Kidderpore Dock, but our orders had been changed to moor in the river. Under normal circumstances this would be no problem, but with the Hooghly bore expected within two days extra precautions had to be taken. Anchor chains were required to be secured to large buoys fore and aft. Hanging off both anchors, and 'breaking' the heavy chains, so that lengths could be lowered into a large barge which was led aft was a long and laborious job.

There was no air-conditioning, of course, and my cabin situated in the main deck alleyway next to the engine-room bulkhead! Even with the temperature at 100 degrees and similar humidity, it was unwise to open a porthole with the hordes of stevedores passing back and forth outside, and with every intention of stealing anything they could lay their hands on. The amount of pilfering that took place in the vast cargo holds was incredible. Despite the attention of sheikh watchmen and frequent visits from ship's personnel, cartons and crates were prised open and their contents strewn around the holds. Some valuable cargoes fared better in the various lock-ups, but after a visit to the Indian continent the amount of pilfered and damaged cargo was enough to fill a large house

To work the five hatches required at least five gangs of stevedores, sometimes more, and together with winch drivers, tally clerks and watchmen, they numbered well over a hundred. During 'smokos', meal breaks, stoppages for rain, they would squat down wherever they could, shouting at the tops of their voices, whilst chewing betel nut and spitting the staining red juices all over the decks. Their personal habits left much to be desired, the strong odour of curry and urine remained long after tour departure from those shores.

And yet, as I had found upon my first visit to India, there is a great fascination about that country which will surely draw me back again one day.

Loading for the Andamans; Howrah bridge in distance

Towing the hardwood logs to the mud shute, Andamans

... for discharge, Dundee

After one such visit to India discharging our general cargo as usual at Colombo, Madras and Calcutta, we received orders to proceed to the Andaman Islands. These islands set in the middle of the Bay of Bengal, were well off the beaten track and were to be another first among my voyages of discovery. We anchored close inshore off the port of Mayabunda. Dense forest towered above, and the valuable hardwood logs, so heavy that they had to be supported by bamboo rafts, were towed slowly out to the ship. *Cannanore* had two sets of derricks each capable of lifting ten tons, but it was all they could do to lift each massive log, streaming with water, slowly up the ship's side and into the gaping holds. It was a slow process taking more than a week giving us ample opportunity for fishing trips in the lifeboat and to explore the densely wooded islands nearby. We watched the felling of the timber, and the elephants as they chain-hauled those massive logs to the top of a mud chute. There with gentle persuasion from tusk and trunk, the log was positioned and pushed and, gathering momentum, rushed headlong to the sea hundreds of feet below.

The Andamans used to be a penal colony for murderers and other serious criminals from the Indian mainland. Perhaps that is one reason why it remains one of the unspoilt parts of the world.

Another visit to the Philippines was to follow. I had long been fascinated by the skill displayed by local fishermen as they skimmed over the water in their fragile outrigger canoes, simply constructed from hollowed out tree trunks, supported each side by a bamboo outrigger, and powered by flour sack sails. I couldn't resist making an offer for one. To my astonishment my offer was accepted. The price? Three bottles of whisky! Strictly illegal, but a bargain for a fully rigged 13 foot canoe with 11 foot outriggers. I launched it ar several ports in the Far East, and when we eventually reached Southampton, the port came to a standstill as the strange craft was lowered into the Solent for her eighteen mile journey to her new port of registry – Keyhaven.

* * *

Salmara was being fitted out for her maiden voyage when I joined her on Clydebank in the winter of 1956. She was a new design of cargo ship with three large bipod masts forward of the bridge which severely restricted visibility and was powered by the largest six cylinder Doxford engine yet fitted in a cargo ship.

After trials and the measured miles off Arran, we loaded in Rotterdam and London before commencing the long haul to China. With the Suez Canal closed it was a very long haul indeed amounting to 14,000 miles. With brief stops for bunkers it should have taken six weeks, but it proved to take much longer.

The heavy engines were producing such vibrations that they caused leaking joints and fractured fuel lines. Time after time the engine-room telegraph rang 'Stop', the alarm bells sounded, and the cursing engineers were on their way below to sort out yet another problem. Each unscheduled stop would take

Salmara on trials. The measured mile off Arran

between 6 and 12 hours, and in that first year alone *Salmara* achieved an unenviable record of 60 breakdowns. For the bridge watch there was little to do except to hoist the appropriate NUC (Not Under Command) signals, while the engineers sweated below. In the Indian Ocean we overtook the same ship on three consecutive mornings having been broken down each preceding night. Our companion must have been impressed at the size of the P & O fleet!

After the stop-start *Salmara* it came as a welcome change to join the troop ship *Empire Fowey*, 19000 tons. She was managed by P & O on behalf of the Ministry of Transport. Based at Southampton her job was to ferry troops and their families to and from the Far East. Built as the *Potsdam* by Blohm & Voss in 1935, she had been one of Hitler's 'strength through joy' ships, with a massive painting of the Fuehrer surmounting the main staircase. Now reconditioned in 1950 by Alexander Stephen, Glasgow, she had accommodation for 1700 passengers and 350 crew. A very popular ship as the return trip to Hong Kong was only two months with a fortnight's 'turn round' at Southampton in between. There was no cargo to worry about, just the regimental baggage which was in the charge of the service personnel.

On one trip we transported a battalion of the Black Watch to Tobruk. Though it was November the weather was warm and the sliding glass doors of the dining-room, situated unusually on the boat deck, were drawn back, providing an ideal setting on St. Andrew's night as the lone piper made his way among the tables followed by stewards bearing the haggis.

If *Empire Fowey* did have any fault it was to be found on her bridge. Instead of the conventional steering wheel she was fitted with a pair of press buttons that must have been revolutionary in the 1930s. Whereas a normal wheel could be turned hard over to hard over in quick time, the press button would not be hurried, taking 34 seconds to achieve the same. No problem once one had become used to it, but for the Suez transit especially, pilots hearing of the impending arrival of *Empire Fowey* would suddenly go sick or take leave! The long convoys, sometimes thirty ships, steamed at 8 knots, a quarter of a mile apart, through the 108 mile narrow cutting through the desert. Some pilots would leave the helmsman alone for as long as the ship was in the middle of the canal water pressure on each was equal and steering easy, but too near one brought a 'yaw' towards the other side. A wheel could correct this quickly, but not the press buttons. More than one nervous excitable pilot lost control of the situation. Too near the left bank, he would rattle off a chain of orders. "Starboard 10, starboard 20, hard astarboard, midships, hard aport." By the time he had given the last order, the button's signal to the steering motor at the stern above the massive rudder had only reached 'starboard 20'. And so the ship would wander from side to side in ever increasing yaws. And not for the first time her bows would push into the canal bank whilst the stern slewed round into the opposite bank, blocking the canal. Ships close astern had to come to an abrupt halt to avoid collision. In subsequent convoys, *Empire Fowey*, in disgrace, was demoted to the back of the queue under tug escort.

Empire Fowey

Chapter Four

Surat Aground

In the 1960s, P & O-Orient Lines operated a mixed fleet of both cargo and passenger ships. The 17 cargo vessels operated three services, to India, the Far East and Australia. The latter was the favourite, and the Indian run the least popular where the 'turn round' in Calcutta might last three weeks with perhaps the South West monsoon adding to the discomfort. The hardest worked were the half dozen 'S' Class cargo ships on the Far East run. The eleven passenger ships offered a world-wide service as well as seasonal cruises from the United Kingdom and Australia. One might spend a year or so serving onboard the flag ship *Canberra* before being brought down to earth on his next voyage, checking the bilges of a cargo ship in Colombo! But the system worked well, and most of us preferred the change to being stuck on one ship too long.

I joined *Surat* in London loading for Hong Kong and Japan. We left the Thames with a full cargo and a full complement of twelve passengers, including the recently retired Royal governess, Miss Peebles. Her introduction to Captain Freddie Irons at dinner that first evening was to leave a lasting impression on her. With the 'old man' was seated at the head of the table and six passengers either side of him, the soup was served and Freddie started his. Miss Peebles sat demurely on his right, waiting patiently.

"What are you waiting for? Get tucked in girl, we don't stand on ceremony here," he said.

"Would you please pass the pepper and salt, Captain?" she asked.

Captain Irons was eccentric, superstitious, and, though kind at heart, possessed of a fearsome temper. The cadets in particular lived in dread of him and made themselves scarce whenever he was about. As his navigator, I soon became used to his idiosyncrasies and his corrections to my courses laid off on the charts.

Coasting in the Red Sea

If I chose an alter course position 5 miles off a lighthouse or headland, he would take great delight in changing that course line with thick pencil to one mile off, and often very much less! I received the rough edge of his tongue one evening when informing him of the sighting of the sliver of new moon just above the western horizon. He rushed to the bridge anxious to turn the money in his pocket and went apoplectic when I pointed through the bridge window! "Never do that again," he roared, moving out to the bridge wing for a clear view, by which time crescent had disappeared. "Let me know if you see it again." Moments later I 'phoned again that the moon was visible. He squinted into the west and shook his head. "Perhaps you need glasses, sir." But I hadn't seen it either!

And so down the Red Sea with the usual call at Aden for bunkers before the long haul to the beautiful island of Penang. Christmas was spent at sea with the ladies much in demand at the wardroom parties. Then followed Singapore, Hong Kong, and then course was set for Japan.

At 5 a. m., as we approached Hokkaido, the southeast corner of the island appeared on the radar, and a good fix obtained from Yerimo Zaki point twenty-eight miles distant. P & O's *Surat* was six miles east of 'dead reckoning' and course altered accordingly direct for Kushiro some hundred miles away. A beautiful mid-winter morning dawned, flat calm, and as the sun rose from the sea it illuminated the snow-clad Tokachi mountains to the north, vivid white against the deep blue beyond.

The ship gradually came to life. The serang and his men busied themselves preparing hatches for loading at Kushiro, in particular No. 3 hatch cooled down for an unusual cargo, a large consignment of frozen cuttlefish which was used as bait for the long-liners fishing the Grand Banks for cod. The seacunnies changed at the wheel. "*Do talli panch, sahib,*" and my Goanese steward arrived with tea and toast, the highlight of the morning watch. In those days, the Chief and 2nd officer shared a steward, while the 'Old Man' had one to himself - how times have changed! Shortly before eight bells, Captain Freddie Irons came up to the bridge and was immediately impressed by the beauty of the distant mountain range which was gradually taking shape on our port bow. Always eager to take a closer look, he ordered, "Steer North, let's take some photographs." With that, he left the bridge on his way to breakfast.

By 9.35 we had closed to two miles off the coast and were running parallel to it along the ten fathom bank. We were due at Kushiro at noon, time in hand, and the scenery was breathtaking. Most of the passengers were out on the boat deck, well wrapped up against the sub zero temperature, admiring the view. At 10.00 it was 'Board of Trade Sports' or, more correctly, General Emergency Stations, a drill which was carried out each week. The ship's whistle blasted, alarm bells sounded, and the crew ran to their posts. Fire hoses were run out, asbestos suits and helmets donned, fire doors and watertight doors tested. Life jackets on, boats swung out and lowered to the embarkation deck. The usual routine, but not easy to fit in when in and out of port almost every day, as opposed to the ample time available on an ocean passage. By 10.30 the

'Emergency' was over and the crew resumed the preparation for arrival, hoisting derricks on the fore-deck, removing hatch securing bars, wedges, tarpaulins - jobs which would have been impossible had the weather been anything less than perfect. The 'Emergency' was over, but another, very real one, lays directly in the ship's path, only minutes away.

On the bridge, the 4th officer and his cadet were kept busy frequently plotting the ship's position The Captain leant over the bridge wing watching the scenery and the crew was busy on the fore-deck. With Kushiro little more than an hour away, the 4th Officer had several other duties to contend with - organizing the flags, pilot ladder, clearing away the anchors, synchronizing the clocks and warning the engine-room. This was normal routine and, of course, his top priority was the safe navigation of the ship.

At 10.34 a fix by visual bearing and radar distance, put the ship inside the line and approaching a two fathom sounding. Under normal circumstances the 4th Officer would have taken immediate action but, with the Captain on the bridge, he chose to inform him first. The Captain walked into the chartroom, looked at the chart, went back to the wheel-house, and ordered starboard helm. The delay was critical. Even as the ship's head began to swing it was too late. With a tremendous tearing crunch, *Surat* impaled herself on a rocky shoal: from full sea speed to full stop in the space of seconds. It took several moments for the awful truth to sink in. Some thought there had been an explosion in the engine-room. Others thought a derrick had fallen. But up on the bridge, the grim reality was clearly evident. For with the main engine still thrashing at full speed, the sea below was calm and still, no longer being thrust aside by the ship's progress.

Perhaps the calmest man onboard was Freddie Irons. He ordered 'Stop' on the engine room telegraph, told the 4th Officer to fix the position on the chart, and picked up the phone.

Surat aground. Ground tackle laid out forward and the 3 Black Balls signal clearly visible

"I'm afraid we're aground Chief, but I want to run the engines at maximum revolutions ahead and then full astern if she's not free."

There were three decks from my cabin to the bridge, but I was up there in seconds, leaning over the bridge wing as the main engine built up to emergency power. There was tremendous vibration as she strained to break free but, after five minutes, it was decided that we might do more harm than good 'Stop engines.' High water had been 0851, but in that part of the world, though there are strong currents, the range of the tide is small, about one metre. There was still a chance to escape before the water dropped further, by changing the trim.

By now reports were coming up from the engine room which was taking water, especially in the 150 foot long shaft tunnel. The watertight door to the tunnel was closed. Water ballast was pumped out of the after tanks and the forward tanks filled to change the trim. The carpenter sounded the bilges, and soundings taken all round the ship to establish the terrain of the sea-bed. "I suppose we'll have to inform London," said the Old Man. "Get hold of the Regulations and Code book, we don't want everyone to know."

Renewed efforts were made to wrest *Surat* from the rock shoal's grip, but to no avail. We were going to need help, and the sooner the better for the weather could change at any time. Mid-winter, and it would need only a moderate swell to grind the bottom out of the ship. Contact was made with the Japanese coastguard who dispatched a vessel from Kushiro. As calm as ever the Captain requested the twelve passengers to assemble in their lounge. He regretted that they would be unable to continue their round trip in *Surat*. Instead they would be landed at a small fishing village nearby, and arrangements made for them to continue to either Yokohama or Kobe, thence to Hong Kong for a scheduled P & O passage to England. But at that stage the passengers were far more concerned for the Captain and expressed their sympathies for him.

The grim reality of the situation was lightened somewhat in the afternoon when a small fishing boat arrived at the gangway to land the passengers. Its decks were littered with large crabs, and it was hard to suppress a smile as Catherine Peebles, the Royal governess, and the others picked their way gingerly among their unwelcome shipmates, and sat on the thwarts with their feet tucked up under their chins! Soon afterwards the coastguard vessel arrived with salvage officials onboard. Bad news travels fast. At the same time we lowered a boat and took further soundings round the ship in the hope in the hope of finding an escape route into deeper water.

As the light faded there was little else that could be done. The passengers were ashore, and the ship and crew in no immediate danger. From within the ship the extent of the damage was impossible to establish. Little did we know that much of the hull from midships to the stern was severely ruptured. Had it not been for the double-bottom fuel tanks and the closed watertight door to the shaft tunnel, the engine room would have flooded and the ship settled more firmly aground, perhaps never to come off. It was an eerie sensation keeping watch on the bridge that first night. A low ground swell rolled *Surat* 5 degrees to port then 5 degrees to starboard, while far below the steady grinding of steel against rock provided a constant reminder of our predicament. There were a few isolated lights from a nearby village to keep us company, whilst high above on the signal mast, three red lights denoted 'Ship Aground'.

At first light salvage tugs arrived, and work began in earnest to lay out anchors ahead of the ship. On the fore-deck all the powerful winches were disconnected from their cargo runners and topping lifts. Massive blocks and tackles were laid out on the deck and shackled to the anchor wires. The preparations were to take three days. Meanwhile tenders for the lucrative repair work were being received from Yokohama, Kobe and Hakodate shipyards. The latter yard was firm favorite being so much nearer, until it was realized that the dry-dock was 10ft too short. "No problem," replied Hakodate, "we shall cut a V in the dock tomorrow."

Another arrival that day was the P & O Superintendent from London. His unenviable brief was to establish the cause, take statements, and sign up the repair yard. A sense of shock pervaded *Surat*. We just could not accept that this beautiful thoroughbred should be rendered helpless and seriously injured. She was our home, had been for months, and we had no thoughts of deserting her now. We'd see it through together. Perhaps we would have thought differently had the weather deteriorated, but it remained calm throughout, and only the low ground swell to remind us of nature's placid mood. There was little else to do but wait. Some wrote letters, and we all discussed at length the 'hows and whys'. A very worried agent arrived from Kushiro. There was a thousand tons of frozen cuttlefish waiting at his port, and now he had no ship in which to load it. But at least he brought our mail, and he promised to post ours upon his return ashore. There had been plenty to write about. There was a letter from Trinity House inviting me to attend an interview for Southampton pilotage within the next six weeks, an opportunity I was now sadly obliged to decline.

For such a tragedy to happen at all, what better place than off the coast of Japan. In recent years Japan had rapidly become the leading shipbuilding nation in the world, and if anyone could re-float and repair *Surat* in record time, it could only be the Japanese. The salvage crew worked day and night laying out the ground tackle 2000 metres ahead of the ship. Then as midday and High Water approached, the foreman stood on the focsle holding aloft two numbered disks marked '5 and 6'. Slowly two large cargo winches picked up the slack of the wire tackle. Then it was '3 and 4', followed by '1 and 2'. Finally it was the windlass that took up the slack on the anchor chain. Gradually adjustments were made to the tensions of each winch, so that each bore an even strain. Then it was the turn of the salvage tug to taughten her tow wire. At exactly 12 o'clock, right on prediction, the foreman, as if conducting an orchestra, raised all six disks, the tug brought to full power, and without a murmur *Surat* began to glide forward.

No time was lost in slipping the ground tackle, and once the ship had been towed into deeper water, the engine was tested and found to be useable despite vibration and the shaft bearings being immersed in sea water. With the tug remaining fast forward, course was set for the few remaining miles to Kushiro where a more detailed survey could be made before the 200 mile passage to Hakodate.

By now our plight had caught the imagination of the Japanese press and television who crowded onboard as soon as we were berthed. With no-one able to speak English, there was no necessity for our 'No comments'. Fortunately there was little concern about pollution for, although many fuel tanks were ruptured, the oil was trapped by the pressure of the water and could only be released once in dry-dock. On the other hand, with the fuel-pipe suctions positioned at the bottom of each tank, it would be impossible to feed uncontaminated fuel to the boilers unless there was one tank watertight. And so it proved. Of the 6 tanks, No. 2 Starboard, containing 153 tons was more than sufficient for the next stage.

Only a superficial survey was possible in Kushiro, and the full extent of the damage could only be ascertained in dry-dock. So we limped on to Hakodate under tug escort with the main bearings running hot in sea water, only to be delayed there for two days with deteriorating weather making it impossible to enter the dry-dock. At last we were secured in the dock and as the water level fell massive wooden posts were wedged in at frequent intervals between the dock walls and ship's sides. Lower sank the water until it reached the chocks upon which the keel of *Surat* rested, four feet above the dock floor.

Only now could the full extent of the damage be appreciated. The hitherto flat bottom was now horribly corrugated and distorted, and a hundred fractures seeped glutinous oil in the sub-zero temperature. Dockyard workers laboured in the awful conditions, hammering in wedges in the attempt to stem the flow. The keel plate, almost an inch thick, as if torpedoed, had a gaping hole 6 feet by 4 feet under the shaft tunnel, and filled with rock, crabs and fish. By now the dry-dock had been pumped clear of water and only the rising level of oil remained as it oozed reluctantly from the ruptured tanks. With temperatures 20 degrees below freezing, the task of clearing up the fuel oil was greatly hampered, and the gangs worked for two nights and days, in acute discomfort and considerable danger, scooping the treacly substance into 40 gallon drums. Over 600 tons were collected in this manner and each change of shift saw blackened figures, covered from head to toe in oil, climbing the steep steps from the bowels of the dock. Then began the unsavory task of cleaning up the dock floor before the cutting equipment could be lowered down.

The damaged plates lying on top of the drydock

We spent many hours crawling through buckled double bottom tanks and bilges making notes as we went along. Everywhere and everything was covered in black slime, and the first jobs up top were to sand the teak decks, lay paper along the internal alleyways and in cabins, and to roll up all carpets out of harm's way. Fortunately, under the circumstances, life went on very much as usual for we were able to use our own generator to provide light, heat and cooking facilities. The P & O Company instructed the Captain to return to London and the remainder were to stand by the ship until repairs were complete. Faced with the prospect of six weeks inactivity, the Nippon Salvage Company more than played their part in keeping us occupied. Each morning a van would arrive, complete with ski equipment, to drive those who were off duty to the slopes of Hakodate Yama, and there most of us were introduced to the sport for the first time

View from the summit of Hakodate Yama

As we gained in confidence, we took our skis by cable car to the mountain top overlooking the port. The views were breathtaking across the Tsugaru Straits where large ferries appeared as small toys as they plied back and forth between Hokkaido and the main island, Honshu. The descent could take half a day, of very much less if one mistakenly followed the routes taken by the vastly more experienced locals, who took great pleasure in trying to teach these strangers the simple rudiments of the sport. We soon perfected the art of baling out if the speed outweighed the courage!

Ice-skating too became a popular pastime, which caused again much amusement among the locals many of whom had never before seen a European, let alone one who was attempting to skate. As on the slopes, there was always someone anxious to help. On one occasion, two engineers who had not brought gloves, and who spent more time falling down than skating, had gloves thrust upon them before their owners melted into the crowd. Another of our engineers, Les Marshall, practiced judo and was welcomed into the local club as if he were a man from outer space. Once on the mat it was a different story, for he was the only member who was not a 'black belt'. His prowess was duly recorded by press and TV until, leaving the club one night, he slipped in the snow and cracked a rib! Also at our disposal was a golf practice net in the repair workshop. There were three cinemas to choose from which regularly showed English-speaking films, but these did not prove as popular as the numerous bars and nightclubs where the pretty Japanese hostesses were only too eager to entertain these strangers from the other side of the world. Several relationships developed, and woe betide anyone who fancied a change, for that would have resulted in loss of face, and all hell to pay!

Our 3rd Officer, Andy Tinsley, established himself into an enviable position. Having frequented the same bar on a number of occasions, he became the apple of the eye of the *mamasan* who appointed him as the bar manager. His job was to keep order, drink as much beer as he could in return for her considerable charms. Another distraction was the organization of 'The Race to the Top' that realized more organizers than entrants. A case of beer was at stake and the umpires took the cable car to the summit where they waited in a nearby café. Several practice runs had proved the course up the mountain somewhat difficult, and by the start that Sunday the number of entrants had been reduced to three standing at the gangway, shivering in the snow that had begun to fall heavily. From that moment no-one saw the other as we chose our separate routes. As we climbed so the visibility decreased, and now, entombed in our own little world, completely lost, there was only one way to go. Eventually we staggered at intervals into the café, somewhat colder than we had been at start an hour earlier. But who had actually reached the summit first it was impossible to tell. The race was declared void, the beer shared, and even vague suggestions of a re-run mentioned.

Meanwhile repairs were on schedule. Large sections of the bottom plating had been cut away together with the contorted steel frames and double bottom tanks. The propeller had been removed and repaired, and the prop shaft re-aligned. At the end of the sixth week, the last of the fifty new steel plates, each measuring 20 foot by 6 foot, had been welded into position. The snows were now melting and the '*sayonaras*' had been said, it was time to go home. After trials, under the command of her new Captain, Roger Cutler, *Surat* loaded a full cargo of cased motorcycles and made her fastest ever passage to London in twenty-one days at an average speed of 19 knots.

Chapter Five

Sunda Multiple Collisions

In the middle of the New Forest near Brockenhurst there is a popular meeting place for model boat enthusiasts. It is called Setley Pond, and here at least twice a week, craft of all shapes and sizes are put through their paces. Some have been made up from model kits whilst others are built from scratch. I watched fascinated as a barque under full sail, came up through the wind, yards braced, before setting off on the other tack. The proud owner, David, is my next door neighbour and his superb workmanship is much admired. It might take him 2 years to complete a 4 foot working model fitted with radio controlled rudder and yards, but launching day always draws admiring glances. Needless to say some of those lining the bank, transmitters in hand, are ex-seafarers, and amongst them were two faces I instantly recognised even though 40 years had past since we last met. We spoke of those intervening years and the different directions our careers had taken. Bob Eaton and Roger Yeatman had read of the grounding of *Surat* in my biography, but did I recall the collisions of the *Sunda* off Dungeness all those years ago when they had both been onboard?

*　　*　　*

On 9 April 1961, Bob Eaton armed with his brand new 2nd Mate's Ticket, joined the 9000 ton *Sunda* in London as 4th Officer. It was here that he met the 2nd Officer Roger Yeatman for the first time. It was Bob's 21st Birthday, but there would be no celebration that busy day as the ship was completing loading and preparing for departure, bound Southampton thence the Far East.

Sunda was manoeuvred with her tugs through the cut into the main section of West India Dock. The voyage got off to a bad start when despite the dock pilot's shrill whistle for the after tug to pull back, and 'emergency full astern' to the engine room, heavy contact was made with the berthed vessel *Temple Hall* causing damage to a lifeboat and davits. Moments later *Sunda* surged ahead again narrowly missing *Mammoth,* the large 200 ton capacity floating crane which was moored at the lay by berth. It was a relief to clear the lock and enter the river, although by now a thick fog had reduced visibility to 20 yards. There was no alternative but to anchor and to await an improvement. After 12 hours *Sunda* resumed her passage down river on the evening ebb, changing pilots at Gravesend. With such an inauspicious start, one would hardly imagine that things could get worse. But they could, and did... Very much worse.

With the Channel pilot onboard and the tight turns of the Lower Hope and Muckings safely negotiated, speed was increased once past the tanker berths of Shellhaven and Coryton. It was an 80 mile passage to Dungeness, and the pilot was pleased to have a fast, well equipped vessel with a good radar, for already there were signs of the fog returning. There was dampness in the air, and the lights of passing ships wore ghostly halos. Captain Porter was making his final voyage to the Far East before retirement, taking his wife with him for a last time. They chatted with the pilot in the wheelhouse before Mrs Porter went below. "Should be at the Pilot Cutter about 3 a m."

Through the narrow Edinburgh Channel, round the North Foreland, and then the Goodwins. By now the visibility had shut in, and *Sunda's* whistle pierced the shrouded night every 2 minutes answering the mournful foghorns of approaching vessels and the neighbouring lightships. Then busy Dover half a mile off, but not a light to be seen. And so on to the rendezvous with the pilot cutter SE of Dungeness. She came in close under *Sunda's* quarter before launching her tender. Meanwhile the pilot bade his farewells on the bridge before being escorted down to the main deck and the pilot ladder.

Soon afterwards at 4 am with the ship 3 miles SW of Dungeness, the Chief Officer David Guthrie arrived on the bridge with his assistant Bob Eaton 4/0 (on his first sea watch) to relieve the 2/0. Within moments, the C/O observed radar echo closing rapidly on a steady bearing on the starboard side. There was no time avoid the inevitable. "Hard a port. Stop Engines. Full Astern."

From the starboard bridge wing Bob peered into the opaque swirling fog. Was it his imagination? Suddenly out of the gloom, a bright green light that seemed to be passing quickly down their starboard side. His immediate reaction was one of relief, the other vessel was surely passing clear. Having just passed 2nd Mate's Ticket he knew each of the many pages of Collision Regulations word perfect, and one little *aide de memoir* immediately sprang to mind 'Green to green, red to red, perfect safety, go ahead.'

But fog plays funny tricks and that green light grew rapidly much nearer, not on a parallel course at all. A large coaster, at full speed, was about to strike *Sunda* amidships.

At 0409 the bows of the *Eva Jeanette* smashed through *Sunda's* side knifing through No. 3 Lifeboat and into the engine room, listing the ship heavily to port. The engineers hardly had time comprehend the situation of grave danger. One moment the bows were embedded in the engine room, the next moment the two vessels had separated, *Sunda* returned to an even keel, and the gaping hole became a raging torrent as hundreds of tons of water entered the stricken ship. Luckily the engineers were able to make good their escape, and the considerable initiative of the 2nd Engineer undoubtedly saved the ship. He had just come off watch and was on deck by No. 4 Hatch for a breath of fresh air. He witnessed the collision and without delay closed the shaft tunnel watertight door.

After the deafening noise of tortured, grinding steel, an eerie silence fell upon the stricken vessel. At least she was upright but was she mortally wounded? Without delay, General Emergency Stations were sounded and a 'MayDay' message broadcast to 'All Ships'. Of the other vessel there was no sign. The 12 passengers and 90 crew were ordered into the remaining boats which were swung at boat deck level ready for lowering. By coincidence, one of the Company's passenger ships *Chusan* was less than a mile astern and she too had just dropped her pilot, but it was considered unnecessary to delay her, as *Sunda* was not then thought to be in immediate danger.

Whilst the carpenter sounded the bilges, Bob Eaton was despatched to inspect No. 4 Hold that was empty prior to loading in Southampton. His torch probed the darkness as he descended the 40 foot vertical ladder to the bottom of the ship. In the gloom he could see the adjoining engine room bulkhead bulging and creaking, with rivets springing under the weight of the rising tide of water beyond. He wasted no time in returning to the bridge with the grim tidings

Meanwhile the tide had set *Sunda* clear of Dungeness, so she could remain drifting without need to anchor until the arrival of a large ocean going tug that had already been contracted by Head Office in London.

There was a moment of light relief amidst the tension when one of the passengers complained that whilst he could endure the considerable discomfort of sitting in lifeboat, he would much appreciate being reunited with his false teeth! This sentiment was echoed by a second passenger and then several more. Once again Bob found himself despatched upon another most unusual duty. He did his best to remember which teeth came from which cabin as he placed them in his pockets, but by the time he'd collected half a dozen dentures they were somewhat muddled up and he had to admit as much on his return as he placed them together on the lifeboat thwart!

Sunda had settled deep in the water on an even keel with no means pumping out the engine-room, but with the emergency generator now providing some light for the accommodation, it was felt safe to vacate the boats and to use the passenger lounge as a dormitory. One officer, refrigerating engineer Tony Gilham, was still wondering whether he was in this world or the next. His cabin had been in the line of destruction, and he had awoken horrified to see the bow come to a halt just inches from his bunk.

But there was to be no peace that night. Suddenly beneath the swung-out port boats there appeared the decks of a vessel so close that the *Sunda*'s crew were obliged to call down warnings and throw buckets onto the intruder. Urgent German voices shouted up in reply and with the clanging sound of their engine-room telegraph, the unknown foreigner edged away into the night.

Needless to say, *Sunda*'s powerful steam whistle was now out of action. It was imperative to activate the Norwegian mechanical fog horn before there were any further close encounters. This was operated by a brass handle that, after but 2 turns came adrift, and had to be replaced by a spanner! Under such circumstances, to accomplish the required fog signal of one long blast followed by two short every 2 minutes, for a vessel 'not under command', required considerable dexterity!

At first light a tug from Dover arrived anxious to put a line aboard and so lay a claim for salvage, but Company arrangements were in hand for the large ocean going tug *Jean Bart* from Le Havre to undertake the tow to Southampton.

The rendezvous was made about 9 am and the tow began soon afterwards, with the tug giving her whistle fog signal followed by the feeble squeaks from *Sunda*. It was to be a difficult job, for as well as the persisting fog, the rudder was still jammed 'hard a port' necessitating the *Jean Bart* to pull strongly to starboard to prevent *Sunda* from veering to port.

With dense fog persisting progress at about 3 knots was very slow. At least the signals from tug and tow would ensure that they were given a clear passage by all other vessels. Or so they thought! Before long they came upon a cautious coaster that had stopped engines upon hearing the approaching tug on his starboard quarter. The Master of *Deo Gloria* breathed a sigh of relief as the tug passed clear, little realising that the tow was not following in the tug's wake. He looked astern to make out the tow at the end of the 100 yard wire. Suddenly directly above him towered *Sunda's* bow with 3rd Officer Hayward shouting down warnings. Water boiled at the coaster's stern as she moved ahead, but not before she had received a sharp nudge in her stern as she disappeared into gloom. But it might have been worse than the 3 buckled stanchions had she found herself caught up in the towing wire as well.

By the light of day, inspection revealed that the davits of No. 1 boat were sheered and might have proved fatal if a launching had been attempted. The tow continued slowly towards Southampton, with the only edible stores available being Guinness, Ryvita and marmalade! Eventually, after 36 hours, they reached the eastern Solent. Four tugs came alongside the now sinking vessel and commenced pumping water out of the engine-room, whilst the Southampton pilot made a careful check of the draft before climbing aboard. With the draft now reading 32 feet, it was 8 feet deeper than on her departure from London. As a result there would now mean four hours delay before there was sufficient water over the Nab bar.

The large tug *Calshott* was made fast on a bridle aft, and with tugs fast on each bow, the tow resumed its sad journey up the Solent. All shipping was halted as *Sunda* and her 7 tugs took up most of the buoyed channel. The big starboard turn at the West Brambles was safely negotiated followed soon after with port swing passing Calshott Spit LV. Bound for the King George V Graving Dock, the largest in Europe, the sooner she took the blocks the better. But *Sunda* had not yet finished her trial by ordeal. As she approached the dock, she took a sheer to starboard, and no amount of correction by the tugs would induce *Sunda* to straighten. Her bows rammed into the coping of the drydock setting the stem back 3 feet. Water cascaded onto the dock from the fractured forepeak tank. Television crews on the dockside awaiting the arrival of the celebrated casualty had a grandstand view of this third and final collision...

Sunda was eventually positioned in the dock, her keel above the blocks, whereupon she literally sank the few remaining feet to the dock floor. It had been touch and go.

Forty-eight hours previously the Chief Officer had commenced the rough copies of Damage Reports by the dim light of the bridge emergency lighting. Within hours he had started on a third one. One can only imagine his thoughts as he picked his way along the drydock wall to view the damaged bow. A fourth Damage Report before they had reached their first port of call to the Far East? Who was going to believe him?

Chapter Six

The Tragedy of *Shillong*

The stranding of *Surat* pales when compared to *Sunda's* multiple collisions off Dungeness, but these events are reduced to a minor key when recalling the trilogy of the 'S' Class disasters: the tragedy of *Shillong*. Whereas *Sunda* (1961) had barely begun her voyage to the Far East and *Surat* (1964) was already in Japan, *Shillong* was half way there, outward bound in the Gulf of Suez.

Having part loaded at several continental ports, before completing at King George V Docks, London, *Shillong,* 9000 tons, commenced her voyage to Japan and the Far East in early October 1957. She was almost down to her marks and was scheduled to discharge at 10 ports during her 'turn round' in Japan, at the same time loading again for the return to Europe. The Chief Officer on those 'S' Class ships was kept fully occupied juggling the mixtures of cargos and their ports of loading and discharge. Stability and trim were also other major factors to occupy his mind. Discipline, maintenance and the 4-8 Watch added to his responsibilities, but ahead beckoned the pinnacle of his career - a command of his own.

It was customary in the P & O, once the Captain and Chief Officer were satisfied with the 4th Officer's competence in assisting with the 4-8 Watch, to promote him to a watch of his own once clear of the heavy Channel traffic and the customary poor visibility, (usually into the Mediterranean). Captain Spurling acted accordingly and Roger Yeatman found himself no longer an understudy, but in charge of his own 8-12, whilst the 3rd and 2nd Officers moved up a watch. For the Chief Officer there would be no more calls - 'One bell, sir, and its a cold miserable night with heavy rain'.

For the 2nd Officer the 4-8 was a welcome change from the 'graveyard' watch. His job as Navigator involved morning and evening star sights as well as the noon position using the sun. And when on ocean passages there would be opportunities to plot future courses, schedules, chart corrections etc whilst his cadet and *seacunny* maintained lookout.

The reshuffle would give the 3rd Officer the 12-4, in addition to which his responsibilities were concentrated on lifeboat maintenance and ship's doctor. With 90 souls onboard, including 6 passengers, his only medical qualification was a First Aid certificate, and his only aid the *Ship Master's Medical Guide*, a large tome showing vivid photographs of various types of venereal disease, what action to take in the event of peritonitis, how to draw teeth and to stitch up gaping wounds...

The ship's company of 84 was composed of 19 officers, 4 cadets, and the usual mixture of Indian deck crew, Pakistani firemen and Goanese stewards. It was an uneventful passage through Biscay, down the Portuguese coast and into the Mediterranean, with a brief call at Almeria for a consignment of grapes. By now the weather was warming up, and everyone looked forward to the Red Sea and the change to 'whites'.

On deck the crew under the hawk eye of the Serang were busy with chipping hammers, combating the ship's worst enemy, rust. Meanwhile those off duty caught up on their sleep, or pursued hobbies, reading, letter writing, cards, scrabble etc. Short-wave radios were popular, as were tape-recorders that were rapidly superseding record players so useless in heavy weather!

For exercise on the boat deck there was shuffleboard, quoits and deck tennis. Swimming pools were sometimes constructed on the aft deck (deck cargo permitting), put together with hatch boards, dunnage, secured by wire-rope and bottle screws, with hatch tarpaulins to hold the water. Better than nothing especially in Red Sea.

But there would be no space for a swimming pool on *Shillong*'s outward voyage. The after decks were stacked high on the port side with heavy machinery, cranes and JCBs, whilst the starboard decks resembled a stable yard with 13 racehorses standing in loose boxes for the uncomfortably long voyage to Japan. Livestock was not an unusual commodity though that number of valuable horses would require the full attention of their groom. If there was an opportunity he would sling them ashore by crane at a convenient quayside en route, for their much needed exercise.

The limited social life onboard was centred round the pre-lunch and dinner cabin aperitifs. It was the way of life in the P & O, and an easy habit to fall in to! In the 1950s, social drinking was encouraged, indeed senior officers on passenger ships were granted an entertainment allowance, even though the price of gin was only 23p a bottle and whisky 35p!

From midday onwards, the question was 'Who's pouring out?' The 'usual' was the cheapest drink, gin & water or a pink gin, as the Company issued the angostura free! Sometimes came an extravagant request for gin and tonic, but as this doubled the cost of the drink, further invitations were not always forthcoming!

It was not until many years later that strict liquor rules were laid down led by the major oil companies after the *Exxon Valdez* grounding in 1989. Breathalysers were then issued to Heads of each department onboard ship, and even the Captain was obliged to undergo a test if a crew member thought such an extreme justified! Drinking is now positively discouraged, and some companies have adopted the American system - dry ships. Though after a long sea passage, much of the crew might become paralytic ashore before being bailed out of jail the following morning by the ship's agent!

*　　　*　　　*

At Port Said, *Shillong* was secured to her buoy moorings, as she awaited other vessels that would make up the southbound convoy. There was the usual mêlée of bumboats busily selling their wares, and on the focsle head a large searchlight was positioned to aid the night passage through the canal. Two boats were hoisted onboard to assist in mooring in transit.

And of course, the 'gulli gulli' man came onboard! He was a great friend of the P & O ships, a jolly, fat Egyptian wearing a red fez and swathed in voluminous robes that housed his stock in trade, baby chicks! He could pluck these chicks out of thin air, or withdraw one from your shirt or even from under your cap. These chicks never left his side, and waited patiently to be gathered up into the folds of his robes, whilst probably wondering where they would reappear next!

That evening, the northbound convoy having cleared the canal, *Shillong* commenced her passage south in the company of 25 other ships. Speed increased to 8 knots with a quarter of a mile gap between each, space enough to pull up if the vessel ahead broke down or ran ashore on either bank. There would be two stops, anchored in the Great Bitter Lake and moored in the Cut, to allow the further northbound convoys to clear. During the transit, Captain Spurling considered that the 2nd Officer was unfit for bridge duties and he was subsequently moved to the 8-12 watch.

Soon after 4 pm the next day *Shillong* was clear of the Canal, had dropped her pilot, and passed the vessels anchored in Suez Bay which would compose yet another northbound convoy. Past Newport Rock and into the narrow Gulf of Suez, the 'Old Man' left the con to the 00W who had a straight run apart from minor alterations for fishing craft and approaching vessels. There were 96 miles to the Ras Gharib light, course 157 degrees. *Shillong* was one of the first in the convoy and was soon winding up to her full sea speed of 18 knots. It was a beautiful evening, and the logbook entry at 2000 hours read 'Fine & Clear. Wind NW/3.'

Among the numerous P & O Regulations there was one quaint instruction still in force which had not been updated since the turn of the century: *'The ship's position is to be worked out every night at 8 pm, and entered in the Night Order Book. At a suitable time after 8 pm, the Chief Officer, having satisfied himself that the fire gear is ready for use, two boats clear and ready for lowering, and that the holds have been visited, will report the same to the Commander and consult with him on the position of the ship and the course to be steered.'*

At 8 pm the 2nd Officer took over the watch, checked the ship's position on the pencilled line he had ruled on the chart whilst the ship was in London. He had drawn the customary diamond shape 2 miles off the Ras Gharib light, and at that point he would bear away 20 degrees to port on to the next course to Shadwan Island.

In the 1950s the navigator had a free hand, subject to the Master's approval, in plotting the courses from port to port. But in areas of heavy concentration of traffic coming from both directions, converging upon their chosen alter course position off a lighthouse or headland, many a close quarter situation arose, especially in reduced visibility.

It was to be some years later that laws regarding the routeing of traffic were implemented in many coastal waters. Then 'each way' shipping lanes with a Separation Zone between them were established, and ships contravening these rules faced heavy fines. Thus for instance, much of the headache of rounding Ushant in fog with 100 echoes on the radar screen was removed. Vessels eastbound followed the one way route off the French coast throughout the length of the English Channel and Dover Straits, safe in the knowledge that the westbound traffic was off the English coast, with a broad Separation Zone between. Haphazard navigation was therefore considerably reduced, and the only concerns, overtaking, fishing and pleasure craft, and the ferries that are required to cross at right angles. But there were no such rules in place in the Gulf of Suez on that fateful evening in October 1957.

The first two hours of the watch passed uneventfully, and the 2nd Officer kept his cadet busy practising chartwork, taking cross bearings with the bridge wing azimuths and checking the distance off the land using radar. The *secunny* was still at the wheel, and the automatic steering would not be engaged until they were well clear of Aden. The lookout was on the focsle head. The Captain would come up with his Night Order Book before he turned in. It was a beautiful, warm, starlit evening. Rig of the day would be 'whites' tomorrow.

Two vessels were observed 10 miles off approaching from the south on a steady bearing a point on the port bow, showing green side lights with their 2 masthead lights slightly open. Both would soon settle onto their new course, and pass *Shillong* comfortably, red to red. In any case the collision regulations were quite clear. It would be those vessels' duty to alter course, and *Shillong* to 'stand on'.

As the two vessels drew nearer maintaining their steady course, the finer of the two crossed *Shillong*'s bow to her starboard bow, while the wider vessel still on *Shillong*'s port bow maintained the same course and collision bearing. As the distance rapidly closed the first seeds of doubt slowly dawned. It only needed a spin of the wheel from that unknown stranger and the danger would pass in a moment.

It was 2225. Surely that ship was going to alter to starboard... Surely... Or was it just a nightmare from which he would awake sweating in a minute? It was far too late for a crash stop 'Starboard' shouted 2/0, and sounded one short blast on the whistle. Almost simultaneously, unbelievably, the vessel ahead had altered her wheel to port, attempting to cross ahead of *Shillong.*

There was no escape now. Collision was inevitable. With violent impact, at full sea speed, the bows of the Belgian tanker *Purofino Congo* knifed into *Shillong*'s port side. The combined weight of 50 thousand tons coupled with the combined speed of 30 knots ripped open a fatal gash 100 ft long. Jack French, Chief Steward, whose cabin was at the point of contact, was killed instantly, as were 2 of the 3 cadets sleeping in their cabins along the port alleyway.

The peace of that beautiful night was now shattered by the strident ringing of the emergency alarms, the hiss of steam escaping from the boilers, and the force of hundreds of tons of water cascading into the gaping wound. The tanker lay astern, stopped dead in the water, anchored to the sea-bed by the length of her cables which had fallen from her split chain locker.

Captain Spurling was up to the bridge in seconds to witness his ship already listing heavily to port. Without delay, he ordered 'Abandon ship. Swing out all boats and prepare the life-raft'.

But the lifeboat gravity davits were designed to operate up to maximum 15 degree list, not twice that amount. The port forward lifeboat was destroyed and the davit of aft port boat, No. 4, was damaged, but eventually the crew managed to free the boat that dropped the short distance to the water. Tragically one of the *ogwallahs* (Pakistani fireman) was caught between the boat and ship's side and was crushed to death.

The inflatable life-raft was manhandled over the lower bridge deck rails with great difficulty due to the increasing list and darkness. Richard Webb, 3rd Officer, taking charge of the passengers' embarkation, was obliged to remove a disabled man's wooden leg before returning to that gentleman's cabin at his urgent request to find his false teeth! Meanwhile 2nd Engineer Derby, braving extreme danger, descended the steeply inclined ladders to the boiler room to shut off main steam.

On the starboard side, desperate attempts were being made to launch another boat. Meanwhile though *Shillong* was settling deeper by the stern, the list was less than it was. Oars were used to lever the lifeboat's keel over the fishplate. At last their efforts were rewarded as the brake was released, and the lifeboat scraped slowly down the ship's side.

In all the confusion, the terror among the horses can only be imagined. The impact and the resulting list must have caused them to fall in the confines of their loose boxes that were not wide enough for them to regain their feet. And what comfort could the groom have offered them? He may well have been as frightened as they were. Perhaps he had the courage to put them all out of their misery. There had been no sound from them.

The remainder of the crew using the ladder and lifelines embarked in the starboard boat (No. 3), and by using the Fleming gear (manually operated levers geared to a large propeller), came clear of the ship's side and in the darkness met up with the port boat with the inflatable raft in tow.

Several ships were now aware of the collision and had stopped at a safe distance. But it was the Danish tanker *Skotland* that took the initiative and came in close to the stricken vessel. Making a lee for the lifeboats, there were willing hands to haul the shocked and bedraggled survivors onboard. They looked across to their beloved ship.

The starlit indigo sky had dimly lit the stage for *Shillong*. The emergency lights began to shut out one by one as the stern sank. The bows raised up, paused briefly before sliding slowly from view. It had taken just one and a quarter hours to reduce an ocean greyhound to but a ripple on the water.

The crew huddled together on the poop deck. Cabin and wardroom sofas were made available as were the beds and the floor in the hospital. Blankets and spare clothing were shared out by the *Skotland's* officers. But sleep was hard to come by with the tragic events etched deep in so many minds.

It was a very subdued crew that disembarked from *Skotland* at Port Tewfik, Suez the next day. They were met by the P & O agent, who had arranged visas with the Swiss Consul. Three days were spent in the shabby Bel Air Hotel under open guard. Coming shortly after Britain's abortive coup against Nasser's seizure of the Canal, the shipwrecked mariners from a British ship were '*persona non grata*'. It was with much relief when they boarded the BI passenger ship *Uganda* homeward bound, the Captain and 2/0 having already flown home for the Enquiry. Passengers were intrigued by the new arrivals in their disreputable clothing, but they were fêted as heroes once the word got round, and bottles of wine were sent to their tables each day.

On the chart of Gulf of Suez, not far from the Ras Gharib Lighthouse, there is a wreck printed 'not dangerous to navigation'. It marks *Shillong*'s grave and a lasting memorial to a fine ship, 4 of her crew and 13 horses.

Chapter Seven

Man Overboard

Of all the P & O ships of the 1960s, probably the most popular among passengers and crew alike was the *Himalaya,* 2800 tons gross with a cruising speed of 22 knots. Built in 1949 by Vickers Armstrong, and first of four replacements for those lost in WWII. Passengers would book many months in advance to avoid disappointment, and it was not unusual for numbers of her 600+ crew to remain for two years or more before signing off on leave. One could detect even when mounting the gangway, that special atmosphere which pervaded the ship. Every effort was made to ensure that the 1400 passengers felt at home. There was always a full programme of entertainment, with libraries and restful lounges for those who preferred the quiet life.

News of gala dances, fancy dress parades, race meetings, films, lectures, quizzes, deck sports and numerous other amusements accompanied the early morning tray of tea. Bridge visits in particular were well supported, perhaps a hundred passengers at a time milling round the wheel-house, chartroom and monkey island. The Engine Room was always warned before hand, for it was not unknown for the E/R telegraph to be mistakenly moved to 'full astern'! Off watch officers took charge of these visits, while the business of navigation was continued by the OOW. *Himalaya* was the first ship to be fitted with photoplot radar, and this fascinated the passengers who were able to keep a photographic record of a passing coastline.

Himalaya was on the Australian run most of the time, though in the summer months she did her fair share of cruises to the Mediterranean, and cruises from Sydney to Japan. These were the 'Cherry Blossom' cruises, and particularly popular with the retired Australians. Sometimes there was too much high living,

Himalaya at her berth. Circular Quay, Sydney

and during one twenty eight day cruise, no less than six burials at sea took place. During one deck cricket match against the officers, a gentleman in his sixties came to the crease, last man in, with forty runs still needed to win. He started to set about the bowling, scored about half the runs, and then collapsed. Much concerned, we gathered round. "I'm alright," he gasped. "Just tell the wife to get the pills."

Five minutes later he was batting again and, slogging the bowling all over the deck, won a famous Australian victory. He collapsed again, and the next morning at 6 o'clock, *Himalaya* stopped, the ensign lowered to half-mast, and after a short service conducted by the Captain, his shrouded body gently slid beneath the quiet waters at the ship's stern. Sad for those he left behind, but we reckoned that he had died happy.

Perhaps it was the succession of popular Captains that helped to build up *Himalaya's* enviable reputation. Certainly Captain Lawrence was in the right mould. He ensured that everything ran like clockwork, and with as little fuss as possible. But he, like many Captains, had his little idiosyncrasies and it was as well to anticipate these. At many ports it was customary to arrive at 0800, and the Captain's Night Orders would include instructions to be called half an hour before the embarkation of the pilot. In reality it meant a deal more than that as I learned as 1st Officer on the 4-8 watch. Arrangements had to be made for his steward to precede him to the bridge with his tray of tea and toast for three, together with a couple of passengers, preferably young and female, to whom he could give his undivided attention while the 3rd Officer and I got on with the arrival routine. I felt somewhat guilty telephoning passengers at 5.30 a.m., but it is always a thrill arriving at a new port, a new country, and they always jumped at the chance. Captain Lawrence looked dashing with his multi-coloured cravat and patent leather dancing shoes, and as long as he had someone to talk to he didn't interfere. Otherwise it was, "Why isn't the house flag close up?" Or, "Get someone to empty this ashtray."

On one occasion, during a visit to Naples, and most people ashore, Captain Lawrence invited one of the WAPs (Woman Assistant Purser) to his quarters for dinner. I enlisted the services of a couple of would be crooners, borrowed a guitar, and after a few hasty rehearsals, assembled outside the Captain's door. What followed can only be described as an excruciating rendition of 'O Sole Mio', several verses, of which we knew only the first three words! In desperation Captain Lawrence opened the door, and with grim face, invited us in for a drink on the condition we continued our Neapolitan song(s) elsewhere. My next invitation to his cabin was in very much sadder circumstances only two days later. Called from the bridge, he asked me to sit down while he broke the news of my father's death. I was devastated, but I shall always remember his gentle compassion and genuine sympathy.

The Crossing the Line ceremony on *Himalaya* was always a special occasion. Not just a haphazard frolic at the swimming pool, but a well rehearsed display to give the passengers something to remember. Half a dozen 'victims' were selected days before who were prepared to enter into the spirit of the occasion.

They were well drilled by King Neptune and his Court, and well prepared for the gruesome fate that awaited them. As we approached the Equator, instructions would be given to throw empty oil drums at intervals from the stern, then the ship steered through three quarters of a circle, gradually, in order not to arouse the passengers' suspicions. Loudspeaker announcements were then made to encourage the sighting of the Line. To add to the realism, violent helm changes would start *Himalaya* rolling, then blasts on the siren, and the news that Neptune and his Court had now boarded. The procession then marched the victims to the pool where Neptune read out the various crimes and penalties to be administered by his 'doctor' and 'barber'. Each victim was lathered and shaved in turn with a large wooden razor before being instructed to lie down on the operating table as the doctor wielded his scalpel. Gruesome scenes followed as strings of sausages, offal and cochineal issued forth in great quantity from the unfortunates' midriffs, whereupon the table top was tilted and the victims slid unceremoniously into the water, into the arms of the waiting policemen who ensured the final indignity of a thorough ducking. The passengers loved it, as did the victims, for their reward was an invitation to Staff Captain Antony Dallas's Neptune party that evening. His cabin would be draped with fishing nets, anchors, shells, cardboard fish, a treasure chest, and in the eerie blue and green light, it looked all the world like an underwater grotto.

So *Himalaya* flew the flag in the best traditions of the P & O until we received news that a new Captain was to be appointed. Captain Walter Eade, RNR, was well known. His recent commands included *Orsova* and *Chusan,* having spent a tough war in submarines. *Himalaya* would have to brace herself. No longer the relaxed atmosphere, but now more like a warship on patrol. It was not unknown for him to arrive on the bridge in the dead of night and instruct the OOW to sound General Emergency Stations. One might well imagine the consternation as the alarm bells sounded shrilly throughout the ship.

His first voyage in *Himalaya* started quietly enough. Fore-warned is fore-armed, and we tried to anticipate him and stay one jump ahead. Then at a fancy dress gala he made his first move. Among the parade before the staff captain and his panel of judges was a young Australian doctor who had contrived to place his severed head under his arm, exposing a neck dripping blood on to the robes of Charles I: a brilliant, if gruesome, effort that won rapturous applause from both panel and audience alike. All except Captain Eade who, standing at the back, sent a steward running to the judges table. "On no account is that fancy dress to be awarded a prize."

Then an event took place that pre-empted Captain Eade, and produced a nightmare situation for 2nd Officer Ian Nicholl sharing his lonely vigil on the bridge with his assistant 4th officer, quartermaster and look-out. It was 2.30 am in the middle of the Indian Ocean during an uneventful passage between Colombo and Fremantle. On the foc'sle head 300 feet away and many decks below, two stewards much the worse for drink, leant over the ship's rail watching the stem knifing through the black water far below. On an impulse one of the stewards clambered over the rails and flung himself over board.

His mate reacted very promptly indeed. Without further ado he ran to the ship's bell situated within yards of him, and shattered the night with its strident ringing. The 4th Officer was immediately despatched to investigate, and moments later a breathless, hysterical steward arrived on the bridge with the news that his friend had fallen overboard. There was no time for delay. Perhaps three minutes had already been lost, and that amounted to well over a mile. For Ian Nicholl there was a series of orders to give almost simultaneously. Flares were released from the bridge wings, and the ship's course reversed in a huge 'question mark' (the Williamson Turn) that would bring her back on the same track. Klaxons sounded for 'Accident Boat' stations, Engine-room and boat's crews alerted, and radio messages to any ships in the vicinity. Despite the urgency of the situation, Nicholl took grim satisfaction when he telephoned the Captain's bedroom to advise him that a 'Man Overboard' procedure was fully in operation.

No sooner had the alarm bells woken me, when my telephone rang. No, I was assured, this was not one of the Captain's jokes, but the real thing. My job was the Accident Boat together with a small crew of six including the Assistant surgeon. We hung there suspended from the davits 60 feet above the water as *Himalaya* eased her speed swinging round on to her new course. A look-out called from the foremast,

"Light on the starboard bow." Eyes strained, then others saw it, a light flare, and then another. Searchlights stabbed through the blackness of the night. The accident boat was lowered, released, and we set off more or less in line with the flares, with our Aldis lamp probing the waters around us. After ten minutes we stopped the engine to listen. It was a beautiful night, but no moon, just a myriad of stars stretching to each horizon. A gentle breeze with a low swell. But just how long could one survive in these shark waters, even if he had survived the fall and the thrashing propellers? I looked across to the gleaming lights of *Himalaya* perhaps a mile away, and it occurred to me that although it looked very reassuring from the comparative security of a lifeboat, what horrible thoughts must run through a man's mind when he floats helplessly in the darkness while his last contact with the life of this world steams over the horizon at 22 knots.

In our imagination we saw ten drowning men as our light reflected the wave tops. We stopped several times, listening, and then, far away, came an unmistakable almost inhuman cry for help. Almost immediately we picked up a struggling figure in our beam. In moments we were alongside, and hauling him aboard. Incredibly we had achieved the almost impossible in rescuing a man from the sea in the dead of night. And as the surgeon administered artificial respiration for he was more dead than alive, I signalled the ship that the man had been recovered and all was well.

No one awaited our return with more concern than a young mother of two who had fallen out with her husband only an hour before. He had threatened suicide, and she was positive that he was about to be returned to her. As the boat was hoisted up the ship's side, she was among the large crowd of late revellers. Imagine her excitement as we drew level, and her despair when she didn't recognise him. A large search party was immediately organised though by now the distraught woman was convinced that she had seen her husband for the last time. Could there possibly have been two overboard at once? The odds must have been several million to one. And so it proved, for a very dejected and drunken man was found huddled in the children's nursery, and reunited with his wife, their quarrel long forgotten.

And so with course resumed for Fremantle, passengers and crew alike returned to their beds. But on the bridge an enquiry was being held. For there was a question that had to be resolved immediately. Why was the rescued steward wearing a lifejacket? He was in no state to answer this himself as he had been drugged and put into hospital, but his mate was interrogated and told several stories which could not possibly have been true. Eventually the truth, as far as we could tell, came out. They had both been drinking, and one had asked the other if he'd ring the fire bell if he jumped overboard. Despite warnings of drowning and the ship's propellers, he'd donned his lifejacket, and jumped thirty feet into the boiling water under the bows. Captain Eade vented his terrible anger on the culprit the next day, when he was logged and fined. But the Captain, always very demanding of the highest standards, had nothing but grudging praise for the smooth handling of the rescue, and from that day onwards we were assured of no Emergency Practice Drills in the middle of the night.

Sad farewells
Departure Sydney

Chapter Eight

'Tripping'

Throughout my seagoing career, interest in pilotage had steadily increased. Despite the disappointment in missing out on Southampton due to our accident in Japan, I was again in contact with Trinity House who had placed me on the waiting list for London, the Cinque Ports Station based at Dover. My fingers were crossed as there were few vacancies, and one's application cancelled if not called by the thirty-fifth birthday.

Meanwhile at each port I had carefully observed the pilot's expertise. Some were better than others. Outward bound again for Calcutta, our first port of discharge was Aqaba. A young Indian pilot boarded to take us to anchor as our berth was not yet available. Rather nervously he conned *Cannanore* into position, but not before he'd managed to touch bottom during the manoeuvre. Nothing serious but enough to merit a casualty report. The next morning the Port Captain, resplendent in a uniform with much gold braid, came onboard with the abject Indian pilot in tow. He berated the poor chap much to our embarrassment, and then set out to demonstrate the art of berthing a ship. We swung out of the anchorage, building up a fair turn of speed, and approached the concrete jetty. We were to berth starboard side to. "Slow astern. Half astern., Emergency full astern," came the orders in rapid succession.

Gradually the speed eased off, but the bows paid off to starboard. It was too late. Our stem smashed into the pier at a broad angle. Concrete flew and water cascaded from the ship's fractured forepeak tank. The stem post was set back six feet. I shall never forget those expressions on the bridge that day. The red faced Port Captain, whose whitened knuckles clenched the bridge rail, the 'old man's' apoplexy, and the young

Indian pilot who stood in the background, not abject anymore. He was having difficulty in keeping a straight face. Another casualty report; this of a more serious nature.

Two months later, as we were completing the homeward loading of tea in Trincomalee, I received my instructions for training as a Cinque Ports pilot. Though excited at the prospect, I thought of all the good years at sea and wondered, just as I had done when leaving Silver Line, whether it was the right decision. However, the advent of the container ship was going to radically change the pattern of life at sea. No longer the leisurely pace of a week or more in exciting foreign ports. One large container ship would supersede six conventional vessels. A busy loading schedule with perhaps twenty-four hours in home port Tilbury, twelve hours in Hamburg, Rotterdam and Antwerp before setting off for Australia without a pause and the same amount of discharge time in Melbourne and Sydney. Now was the time for change. P & O were very generous. "Give it a try," they said, "but we would be glad to have you back."

The interview panel at Trinity House consisted of Elder Brethren and members of the London Pilots' Council. All went well until I broached the subject of pensions. I was critical of the paltry pension, which compared unfavourably with that of P & O, who retired staff on two-thirds salary. But that was the system, take it or leave it! Looking back to 1967, it is hard to believe that a pilots' pension scheme was not already in place, and unbelievable that the shipping companies were not prepared to pay for the training of pilots of the future. 'Tripping' was thus carried out at one's own expense and would last between 4 to 6 months depending on the candidate's previous Thames experience. But now the die was cast and the gold braid earned over the years removed from the reefer jacket. Even the brass buttons replaced by black ones to denote that I was merely a 'candidate'. Once again I was at the bottom of the pile. It reminded me vividly of those other first rungs of the ladder. Those first days at boarding school as an eight year old, the first days at

Warsash, junior cadet on my first voyage, 4th Officer in P & O and now, here I was again. Not even a pilot, merely a 'candidate'!

Ro-ro ship bound Tilbury making the aft tug fast.
Royal Princess in the background berthed at Tilbury Stage

There were four of us 'tripping' at that time, and it was our job to assimilate as much knowledge of the Thames and its approaches as possible before presenting ourselves for examination for Pilot IVth Class. This required at least one hundred trips to or from Folkestone - Gravesend, with additional local trips in and out of Dover, Ramsgate and Whitstable. The license was also to include Richborough and Faversham Creek though ships using these small ports were few and far between. Trips on tugs were also important. There was a lot to learn and it was to be a busy six months.

Pilots' attitudes to candidates varied considerably. A few imagined a loss in their income having to share with the newcomers. Others, approaching retirement with a clean record, were loathe to let a candidate handle his ship. Usually it was the younger pilots, with better memories of their own candidate days, who were sympathetic and encouraged one to 'take the con'. In subsequent years when taking a candidate with me, I have discussed the job before boarding the ship, made it clear that he will be in charge, and then, once onboard give the impression of taking little interest in the proceedings. Afterwards we would discuss any 'fine tuning' that might be required. In my view, it is the only way to instil that vital ingredient - confidence.

With a hundred pilots plus pilots based at both Folkestone and Gravesend, I was meeting new faces every day as I shuttled back and forth. Being an inward candidate, I was not so concerned with the outward work. It was difficult enough learning all the courses, distances, depths, buoys inward, let alone learning it all in reverse as well. Usually an outward pilot would recognize this and permit the candidate to catch up on his chartwork, or perhaps grab forty winks. It was sometimes an embarrassment, having slept

Sunrise. Landing the pilot at Royal Terrace pier, Gravesend

comfortably on the chartroom sofa all the way back to Folkestone, to have one's 'Tripping Book' signed with the customary remarks 'Keen and Attentive!' I found accommodation in Gravesend, and soon discovered that the time of High Water onwards ensured busy outward traffic, especially on Friday nights. This was a direct result of the working methods that existed in the London docks in those days where the stevedores worked a five day week and any ship left alongside her berth at the end of the week would remain idle there until completing the following Monday, an expensive liability for the ship owner who would usually cut his losses by sailing his ship light of cargo in order to arrive at the next loading/discharging port as near to schedule as possible. With work in the enclosed docks ceasing at 1700, the tide was the next consideration when suitable conditions for undocking, both enclosed and riverside, would not occur until half flood onwards.

The repercussions of this mass exodus realized a heavy workload for the Channel pilots based on Royal Terrace pier. There could as many as 50 ships due outward overnight. Communication was sketchy in the '70s, ships fitted with VHF a minority, and it was up to the pilot cutter to have sufficient men onboard to serve ships rounding Tilburyness on a strong ebb. By the time half a dozen ships had changed pilots the cutter might well have reached the Ovens buoy at the bottom end of Gravesend reach, and would then have to beat back to the pier against the tide to collect more for further ships rounding the point. Nor was there any system of 'duty pilot' in those days and nobody to warn you again when the messenger had completed his calls for the night. "Good evening, Mr Bloggs. You are number 37, with the 37th job due down at 0545. In last thing please." During those long nights it was custom to endeavor to sleep in the 'back room' of the pier that was fitted with four double bunks and a dozen settees, but even so it was difficult to sleep through the general comings and goings, phone calls, snoring and restlessness that pervaded.

Inward bound passing Tilbury Power Station

There was nobody to call you, just the man ahead on the roster to give you a shake that he was about to ship. Invariably one would board one's ship tired and irritable for an approaching act of pilotage that might last 12 hours. The object of the exercise was to find myself a suitable ship to get me to Folkestone in time for a transfer to an inward vessel. On one occasion I asked the 'turn' pilot on Terrace Pier if I might join him. "By all means, but if I were you I'd wait for the Port Line ship lowering down in Tilbury lock. She'll be here in half an hour and will soon overtake my coaster." It proved sound advice and perhaps saved my life!

It was a black winter's night, with a roaring ebb tide and a procession of traffic outward bound. Tom Williamson climbed the ship's ladder from the cutter, took over from the river pilot, and set course for the Shornemead light at the bottom of Gravesend reach two miles away. As he made the wide turn into the Lower Hope, another ship overtaking too close, struck the coaster. Over she went on her beam ends and Tom was left climbing to the high side of the bridge, then out on to the ship's side, at the same time struggling in vain to release the bridge wing life-buoy. Quickly the coaster sank beneath him and it was only the prompt action of nearby tugs picking up survivors a mile downstream that loss of life was avoided. Anxious not to alarm Mrs Williamson, for her husband had suffered from a heart complaint, the pilot station phoned her. "Could you bring a change of clothing for Tom? I'm afraid he's got himself a little wet." This job was going to be more interesting than I had bargained for!

About halfway through my training, I found myself thrown into the deep end when joining a large cargo ship outward bound off Gravesend. John Bain had invited me to accompany him on the trip down to Folkestone. He was one who encouraged the 'hands on' approach for a candidate, but I got more than I bargained for, and so did he! John was half way up the ladder when the wash of a passing ship squeezed between the pilot cutter and our ship forcing upwards a solid wall of water that completely engulfed him. I followed him up to the bridge where he was already stripping off his sodden clothing. Soon after he reappeared briefly wearing the captain's dressing gown and told me to get on with the job while he dried out. Passing Dover hours later, John returned and asked how I was getting on. I learned a lot that day!

The outer reaches of the Thames run from the North Foreland to Harwich, but it is not until you reach Southend that the river takes shape. Soon afterwards the oil refineries of Canvey Island, Coryton and Shellhaven are passed to starboard, and thereafter the river narrows considerably. A broad turn to port into the Lower Hope and the Muckings is followed by a right angled turn round Coldharbour Point opening up Gravesend Reach, due west, and into the busiest stretch of the river.

Over the centuries Gravesend became the established point of entry for the Port of London. Customs clearance, Port Health, Immigration, Pilot, tugs. Water and oil barges loading up to serve ships in the river. Numerous berths, repair yards and drydock, anchorages, swing buoys, and the Gravesend - Tilbury ferry.

At the end of Gravesend Reach there is a wide turn to starboard into Northfleet Hope, passing Tilbury Lock entrance, container and grain terminals to starboard, Broadness is now only half a mile away which involves a large 120 degree turn to port. Outward traffic can be seen across the marshes from the bridge of a large vessel, but only the tops of their masts from a small one. The channel narrows on the bend, with the tide setting strongly onto the north shore and the notorious Black Shelf, guilty of many strandings, lying in wait. On the starboard beam as you begin the turn, lies the sad wreck of the unfortunate Gull Light vessel, which spent its retirement as the clubhouse of the adjacent Thurrock Yacht Club. .

In March 1929, *Lightship No. 38* (her official title) was stationed in the Gull Stream off Ramsgate, in place of the regular vessel in need of a refit. Within a week dense fog set in, and the Ellerman liner *City of York* rammed and sank her. The crew was saved, but the skipper went down with his ship. *Lightship No. 38* was subsequently raised and returned to service off Ramsgate. After air attacks in 1940 she was towed to Great Yarmouth, and in 1947 bought by Thurrock Yacht Club for £750.

The wreck of the Gull Lightvessel lying at the Thurrock Yacht Club

Chapter Nine

Trinity House Pilot

And so at long last came qualification as a pilot, IVth Class, earning money even if it was only 50% of the full 'sharing turn'. The first two years were to be limited to vessels up to 2000 tons gross. The four juniors were based on the Isle of Thanet, dealing with small ships bound for London from the near continent and, in addition all the movements in and out of Ramsgate and Whitstable and the occasional visitor to Faversham and Richborough.

For the new boy, Ramsgate posed the biggest challenge and it is amusing to reflect that a pilot with the least experience was thrown into the deep end when bringing a ship into this small port in adverse conditions. The vessel was boarded about a mile off the port and the first job was to reassure the worried Captain, and indeed oneself, that the entrance was not as narrow as he feared! Round the fairway buoy, and then NNE aiming at the port hand pierhead as the strong north-easterly tide swept across the entrance. Some speed had to be maintained for once the bow was inside, in still water, the stern would rapidly close the starboard pierhead. Once inside the Royal Harbour one could sense the Captain's relief, and it was only when shaping up for the narrow lock entrance that he would realize the ordeal was not yet over. The usual practice was to steer her straight through with fenders at the ready and fingers crossed. With the lock negotiated, there was another tight turn into the Inner Basin and then, at last, the berth.

Today Ramsgate is unrecognizable. The once beautiful Victorian port has been spoilt by the construction of massive concrete breakwaters to accommodate the occasional ferries. At long last a suitable road link has been built, before which forty-ton container lorries would thunder through the streets twenty-

South Quay, Whitstable, with the fish dock in the foreground

four hours a day. Both the Inner Basin and the Royal Harbour is now a yacht marina, with Ramsgate Week is becoming increasingly popular on the racing calendar.

Europa leading the tall ships out of Ramsgate. The last vessel has just cleared the lock leading to the inner basin

The approach to Whitstable via the Street Buoy, and the unlit Slavery buoy was straight forward enough, but the harbour entrance is narrow and sufficient speed is required to maintain steerage way. This is another tidal port that, like Ramsgate, almost dries out at low water springs, but can accommodate a draught of about 4 metres at High Water. The ideal time of entry is an hour before this, after which the tide begins to ebb across the entrance. At night, with the lights of the town behind, it is difficult to identify the pierheads until quite close, and on occasions, with vessels moored on both East and West quays, there is little room to squeeze through. Bare steerage way, and then 'full astern'. My very first trip there required a casualty report and a visit to Trinity House to explain heavy contact with the South quay!

Beyond Whitstable and into the Swale, lies the entrance to Faversham Creek. Here the pilot, having boarded his coaster off Margate, would hand over to the local boatman for the meandering miles up the narrow creek to that beautiful little port and favorite haunt of artists.

Vessels bound for Richborough were very rare indeed, and the pilot would need to have a close look at the chart of Pegwell Bay before he embarked. It dries out at Low Water except for a narrow winding stream marked at intervals by wooden stakes. Once in the river and approaching the berth to starboard, the theory was to steer the bows into the mud of Stonar Cut and let the last of the flood bring the stern round, but not such a good idea if the vessel should get stuck athwart the river. During the First World War, Richborough answering the call to arms was developed into an important train ferry port complete with rail sidings and gantry cranes for loading the barges purpose built there to fit the dimensions of the French locks. Further innovation by the Royal Engineers were the containers which were loaded directly from the wagons on to the barges. Was Richborough was the first container port?

Although a junior pilot would have become familiar with the port of Dover during his 'tripping' days, by the time he graduated from the Thanet station into the main roster based at Dungeness/Folkestone, he would be somewhat rusty on his first solo trip. Passing through the busy Eastern or Western Entrances, most of the commercial traffic would be bound for the enclosed docks at the western end. The lock gates open about 2 hours before HW at which time there is a strong tidal set across the Prince of Wales pier. Once through the Wick, the Granville Dock lies ahead with the Wellington Dock and swing bridge round the corner to starboard. There is a constant stream passing through the Wellington from the Dour river, and a vessel feels the set to port as she approaches the Granville lock entrance with fenders at the ready. There is little over a ship's length to pull up once inside the dock. Nor is there room to turn for vessels over 285 feet, and these have to enter stern first with tug assistance aft and two mooring boats fast forward.

The picturesque harbour of Faversham at low tide. Having come through the Swale, the rendezvous with the local boatman was at the fairway buoy marking the entrance to the winding creek

The Dover ‘Look Out’ was situated in Marine Court with a fine view overlooking the harbour, and across to Calais on clear days. The Dover watch was set each morning separate from the main roster, and the two pilots would deal with the movements within the port and any continental work for London. An order for a ship requiring a pilot in Antwerp bound London for instance, would mean a ‘stand off’ for the first man with the second taking his place.

For many years the French train ferries in and out of Dover had required compulsory pilotage and it was more expedient and cheaper for the pilot to do the round trip to Dunkirk than to disembark once clear of Dover. He had little to do other than to communicate with Port Control on VHF, advise the Master of shipping movements in and around Dover and then to ‘stand down’ once clear of the South Goodwin LV and outside pilotage waters.

Occasional ferry pilotage made a change from the normal run to the Thames, but with the introduction of new ferry services, heavy inroads were made on the pilot roster especially in the 1980s. Then Olau Line introduced a twice daily service from Ramsgate to Dunkirk before moving to Sheerness with large vessels on the Flushing run. Meanwhile Sally Line established itself at Ramsgate with a passenger service to Dunkirk, as did Schiaffino Line with lorries and their drivers to Ostend, and the P & O Jetfoil service from St Katherine’s Dock to Zeebrugge (later changing to Ostend). All these services were required to carry pilots, and as many as ten might be ‘ferrybound’ at the same time.

But in 1988 it was all change when government legislation required CHAs (Competent Harbour Authorities) to become responsible for their own pilotage areas. The Cinque Ports Pilots, having operated an efficient service for four and a half centuries, would now become employees of the Port of London Authority, whilst Dover Harbour Board called for four volunteers. Since that time Dover has seen many changes especially in the increase in size of the ferries, the number of large cruise ships and increased imports in the fruit trade.

Trinity House vessel *Patricia* passing through the Wick, approaching Granville Dock, Dover.
The Prince of Wales pier in the background

Early in the 16th century there was growing concern for the safety of merchant ships plying the Thames. Many a vessel had come to grief at the hands of bogus pilots who had steered their victims into some prearranged rendezvous of shallow bay or rocky foreshore, where wrecking gangs stood by to unload the cargoes through the night or under the blanket of fog. There was concern too over the number of foreign vessels discovering the secrets of the river. If the shoals could be charted in peacetime, then it would not be too difficult for an enemy fleet to attack the very heart of London. At this time local houses of charity for distressed seamen had been built and named after the Holy Trinity as Trinity houses. Among the volunteers who ran these establishments were some with nautical experience such as retired captains and fishermen. They were invited to form a select group of pilots under the Charter of 1512 issued by Henry VIII. Thus was the Trinity House pilot born.

In 1808 a cruising cutter was established off Dungeness that became the rendezvous position for London bound ships. Pilot numbers were topped up to 14 morning and evening by tender from Dover.

Last on the list in bad weather and no ships due could mean several uncomfortable days of waiting. But for me, 1967 was a good year to join the service. This brought about the demise of the Dungeness cutter and the advent of the fast launches operating out of Folkestone harbour, and requiring only 3 pilots on standby in a luxurious new building.

Though licensed for the Thames district, there was an additional attraction in obtaining a Deep Sea certificate. I was examined at Trinity House for the area Brixham to the Elbe, and this added variety ensured the job was never dull. Although opportunities for this 'outside' work were few and far between, the charts required frequent correction from the weekly editions of Admiralty Notices to Mariners. The North Sea charts in particular required checking from week to week, what with the gradual clearance of minefields off the Dutch and German coasts, the rapid establishment of oil fields off the British coast, the laying of pipelines, construction of wellheads, rigs under tow, and all requiring plenty of sea room.

One such voyage was onboard the deep draft tanker *Conoco Espana*, Brixham bound Humber. It was a fine morning as we picked our way through the maze of drilling platforms that were mushrooming in the Indefatigable and Leman fields. Suddenly a shattering explosion from the engine-room disturbed the peace of the forenoon watch - and total breakdown. A generator had blown up and an engineer was seriously wounded. Luckily, no sooner had we called for medical assistance on VHF, than a helicopter was dispatched from a nearby rig. A medical orderly was tending the wounded man within fifteen minutes of the explosion, before being whisked off to Ipswich hospital and a full recovery.

Under pilotage off the North Foreland. Tug *Switzerland* towing *Stirlingbrook that* had broken down off Le Havre (November 1982)

Then came another call to Brixham to join a Brazilian warship bound for the Elbe. Even though it was 550 miles, I looked forward to a fast passage. When I arrived at the pilot station, bad news, already 24 hours late, and only making 8 knots. Instead of speed, I had to be content with a large self-propelled floating drydock. It proved to be a very long trip, especially as the bridge team was highly nervous of the Dover Straits and loath to allow me any time for rest!

My longest trip was onboard a new Japanese cargo ship bound for Oskarshamm on Sweden's east coast. Having boarded at Brixham I had intended disembarking at the Skaw (off the northern tip of Denmark), but the Captain was anxious to extend my services to his destination even though this was well beyond the terms of my license. I checked that his charts were up to date, and off we went - into a wall of dense fog! I soon realized that the bridge team had little or no experience of poor visibility and the suggestion of a radar plot drew blank stares. Engines to standby was understood, but the need for an extra lookout on the foc'sle head was not. When he did eventually go forward he was deafened by the typhoon whistle situated twenty feet above his head, so he was hurriedly moved to the bridge where none of us could see the foredeck anyway!

Once clear of the Dover Straits, the visibility improved and I was able to snatch forty winks and another break when we embarked the local pilot off Halsingborg for the narrow Oresund passage between Denmark and Sweden. Thence into the Baltic, north again round Oland and, at last, our destination. I was relieved to find that we would not berth until the morning, time enough for a good night's sleep before flying home.

Japanese tanker *Saiko Maru* 48000 tons gross 43 ft draft, at anchor near the Sunk anchor near the Sunk Lightvessel awaiting the beginning of the flood before proceeding inward for Coryton

Cuban *Bahia de Puerto Padre on passage Brixham to London. Fine weather S/8*

Thames barges racing in the Sea Reach off Southend

Rochester Barge
South Foreland.
23. VI. 80.

Maersk Kent outward bound (top)   First of the ebb at Southend

The radical changes in pilotage of 1988 in the Thames when pilots no longer enjoyed self-employed status, has produced a more streamlined service. Instead of separate stations at Harwich, Ramsgate and Gravesend, there is now one roster and consequently the work is now more diverse. One 'turn' might entail the passage of a large tanker from Littlebrook Power station (Dartford Crossing) to the Sunk Light Vessel off Harwich, the next a small coaster from off the North Foreland to Purfleet. A lot of travel is involved, but a fleet of cars is at hand to ensure the 'turn' is completed without delay. From *Royal Princess* to river barge, flat calm to storm force, clear as a bell or thick as a hedge. Where to? Where from? One cannot complain that the job is ever dull.

Despite the many changes at sea which have taken place in the past twenty years, the demise of the British merchant fleet, the advent of the flags of convenience, third world crews, the increase in size of ship and draft, the act of pilotage has changed little, unless one is to whisper that with all the improvements in radar, communications, speed and manoeuvrability, the job has become, if anything, easier. We do not share the considerable commercial pressures that now weigh upon the Master. The pilot's only focus is to ensure the safe passage, and to remove any factors that might obstruct this. The pilots of old were, in many respects, more accomplished than today's. They might turn in their graves at the size of the modern vessel but we in turn would blanche at the thought of navigating a ship in the Thames estuary with no radar or VHF radio and only a magnetic compass and sounding lead as our guide, peering into the gloom from the cold bridge wing for the next buoy and listening for its bell. Nowadays, within the comfort of the enclosed heated wheelhouse, it requires only a cursory glance at one of the radar consoles to reassure what one knows already. The VHF is at your side and the coffee percolating nearby.

Then in 1989, for a brief exciting week, the clock was turned back a century. It was London's turn to host a visit of the Tall Ships, and an opportunity to experience what it must have felt like bringing large sailings ships up the river. Off Southend, I boarded the large Spanish training vessel *Juan Sebastian de Elcano* bound for the Pool of London. She was a four masted top-sail barquentine of 3,754 tons displacement and 113 metres in length. With 350 crew onboard, mainly cadets, she was a magnificent sight as we progressed slowly through the estuary under full sail, but with considerable help from her engine in the light winds.

The next day I had a rendezvous off the North Foreland with the Portuguese training schooner *Creoula.* She appeared on the horizon under full sail in the fresh NE'ly breeze. But as we approached in the pilot launch I was disappointed to see the sails being sent down. Once aboard I expressed my opinion that we would make better progress under sail again than with the small noisy diesel engine. 'Full and bye' we made excellent time until we entered Gravesend Reach where once again under power, we berthed overnight at the Tilbury stage. *Creoula,* a four masted fore-and -aft schooner began life fishing the Grand Banks off Nova Scotia and Newfoundland. She carried fifty-four sixteen foot dories which were launched at dawn, each with a single fisherman equipped with a mile of line and a thousand baited hooks. At the end of the day the boats, almost swamped with the weight of cod, would sail back to the mother ship. Once onboard, the fish were gutted, salted and stowed away in the holds. The season lasted from March until October when with a full load of 800 tons, *Creola* returned home to Lisbon. But such were the dangers of this life that the Portuguese government imposed a ban in 1973.

Chapter Ten

The Boeing Jetfoils

No two acts of pilotage are the same. There are so many ingredients involved - weather and tide, type of vessel, speed and draft which will determine which route to take, and where bound. Perhaps the deep water jetties of the oil refineries at Thameshaven, or perhaps the other extreme, a small place such as Gibbs Wharf which dries out and can only be negotiated at high water. Anything between the eight-knot schyte and the eighteen knot container ship was the kind of ship to expect.

Then P & O introduced a pair of Boeing jetfoils on a new service to run between St Katherine's Dock and Zeebrugge. Twin 3,700 hp gas turbine engines produced a powerful water jet at 200 tons per minute to force the craft out of the water and on to its foils. The result was a fast and comfortable ride for the 280 passengers. There were drawbacks. The North Sea crossing could be hazardous and a three metre swell as much as the craft could handle. Another factor was, although when up on her foils the draft was a mere five feet, it was essential to operate in depths of at least twenty feet in case a breakdown brought the hull suddenly down onto the surface without time to retract the foils. Such a depth was not always available at low tide in the upper reaches of the Thames. Consequently arrival at St Katherine's could be forty minutes late much to the consternation of passengers who had been flying up the river one minute and then down onto the hull at 8 knots for the remainder of the passage. Departure cancellations too would cause annoyance among passengers awaiting embarkation, for a bright sunny day in London did not reflect the unfavorable conditions that might exist in the Thames estuary.

For a pilot attached to a jetfoil, the return trip to Zeebrugge made a pleasant change to conventional piloting. The forty-two miles from Gravesend to the North Foreland was achieved in less than an hour, and upon arrival at the Belgian port he would be chauffeured to a pleasant hotel in nearby Bruges for the overnight stop. On one such stopover the weather had deteriorated by morning. The wind had increased to force 8 WNW and had already brought hovercraft services to a halt and disrupted ferry schedules. I had resigned myself to a day exploring pleasant Bruges when the jetfoil captain, an American who was also the Boeing test pilot, arrived and suggested we take a closer look at conditions at the port. Large waves swept the breakwater and the wind was increasing. Even to consider departure was out of the question.

But I had reckoned without the Captain. He had made his mind up. Too risky for the passengers waiting in the terminal so arrangements would be made for them to fly. He was determined to test his jetfoil's capabilities. I protested, but he just could not resist the challenge. "Let's see what she really can do."

There is just enough room in Zeebrugge for the 1000 foot take off, but by the time we had cleared the entrance, strapped into safety belts and holding on for dear life, the wave tops were as high as the bridge. Almost immediately, at 35 knots, *Jetferry One* smashed into a wall of water and was knocked down shuddering onto her hull, wallowing in the troughs. Undeterred the Captain drove her up again with the gale abeam and using the troughs to gain momentum. Up on the foils again we raced over the waves trying to keep the vulnerable craft at a constant height up and over the swells, but to no avail. Another solid wall smashed onto the hull with tremendous force and again we were brought abruptly to a halt. By now we were drifting we were drifting perilously close to the shallows of the Ruytingen Bank. Time and again the jetfoil was forced up onto her foils, the water jet building her speed to thirty knots and more. With the wind abeam she rode the heavy swell, but each time we turned away from the lee shore, came another knockdown. We were running out of options and sea-room. Battered and bruised we had to admit defeat and return to the safety of Zeebrugge.

We arrived eventually having suffered twenty knockdowns, sadder but much wiser. P & O ceased operations soon afterwards and the two jetfoils were transferred to the Dover - Ostend service in conjunction with conventional ferries. Thus, even if the jetfoils were weatherbound, passengers were still able to make the crossing. Then in January 1994 with the Chunnel opening that year, the Belgians transferred their operations to Ramsgate.

Chapter Eleven

A Close Call

Jim Francis was a newcomer to the pilotage service, having recently been appointed by Trinity House to Cinque Ports, the Southern arm of the Thames district. As a junior pilot his duties embraced any movements of shipping in and out of Ramsgate and Whitstable, and to serve ships making night-time rendezvous off the Thanet coast bound for London.

There were 100 Cinque Ports pilots based at Dover and Folkestone, with the four juniors stationed on the Isle of Thanet ready to move quickly, and also to deal with any ships giving no ETAs. The pilots prided themselves on a very efficient service. Ships were not to be delayed. There was further incentive in those self-employed days of the alphabetical roster. If the pilot 'on turn' could not be found, his turn was lost and the 'job' went to the next man.

The winter of 1962/3 was the severest for many years with snow and ice persisting for 3 months. The early hours of February 1st was no exception, and upon his arrival at the port of Ramsgate soon after midnight, Jim noticed that the ship for which he had been ordered, the *Weserstrom*, was enclosed by ice in the Inner Basin. There were numerous ice floes in the outer harbour, and pack ice was piled high in the harbour entrance. But there were patches of clear water, and Jim decided that it was safe enough to proceed to sea.

Outer Harbour, Ramsgate, February 1963

Weserstrom was a typical German coaster of 499 grt, and the manoeuvre in calm conditions, despite the ice, would present no undue difficulty for Jim. Out through the narrow lock, a sharp S bend through the harbour entrance, and then, once clear of the Quern shoal, down the ladder into the waiting pilot boat and back on dry land in half an hour. That was the theory, but events that took a completely different course

Having negotiated the narrow lock, it requires a cool nerve to build up speed whilst heading for the eastern breakwater before turning hard a starboard, through the entrance and into the NE going tide. Soon afterwards Jim had cleared the Quern shoal and brought *Weserstrom* in a tight turn to port in order to provide a lee free of ice for boatman Bob Cannon who had been following in his wake. "Stop Engines".

Jim shook hands with the Captain, wished him "*Bon voyage,*" and was accompanied by a crewman down to the maindeck, where the pilot ladder had been rigged for the 15 feet descent into the boat. Bulwark steps with a pair of stanchions, had been placed against the ship's side. Jim mounted these and grasping the stanchions firmly, turned and felt for the first rung of the ladder. In a fleeting moment, and too late, he realised his weight had levered the bulwark steps off the deck. He fell backwards into a sea of ice with steps and stanchions on top of him.

The numbing cold and darkness focussed Jim's mind as he struggled to the surface. He was a young, fit man but he knew there was little time. Already he had been swept clear of the harbour lights, and whilst the tide flowed strongly, his strength was ebbing fast. Bob Cannon had quickly assessed the gravity of the situation, but it was to be several minutes before he could manoeuvre his boat to the drowning man still enmeshed in the steps and ice.

Bob put the engine in neutral and leant over the gunwale in a vain attempt to haul the 14 stone, 6 feet pilot aboard. But Jim was literally freezing to death. His heavy clothing and boots were weighing him down, his senses numbed. Immediate action was essential. The boatman passed a rope under Jim's arms, made it fast to a cleat, and towed the half-submerged, stiffening figure the half mile back to Ramsgate.

Meanwhile Ramsgate hospital had been alerted. As soon as the boat came alongside the jetty with its valuable tow, willing hands carried Jim up the steps. By now his body was frozen and unbending, and it was impossible to lever him into the waiting car. Without delay a van was commandeered, and the journey achieved in record time. The clothes were cut from his body and he was placed in a cool bath, and slowly brought up to body heat. A warm bed, two hours sleep followed by a hearty breakfast, Jim felt fully recovered and told Matron so.

She was not so easily convinced. "No, Mr Francis, we shall keep you in for observation for 24 hours. And anyway, you've got no clothes. They're still soaking wet!"

But after further persuasion, both Matron and Doctor relented, and granted him permission to return home to Dover in hospital dressing-gown and pyjamas. A taxi was ordered, and a much relieved Jim set off down the corridors, a rather bedraggled figure, carrying a sodden, dripping bag of clothing!

At the main entrance, the hall porter cast a critical eye at this strange apparition. "May I ask where you're off to, sir?"

"Oh, it's all right, I've been released. I'll be bringing the hospital clothes back tomorrow."

The porter was not impressed. Grasping him firmly by the shoulder, he marched a protesting Jim back to the ward. Jim smiled grimly to himself as he compared his present situation to that of only three years ago when he had been in command of his own ship in the Union Castle Line.

Meanwhile in Dover, Mary Francis, mother of two small children and shortly expecting a third, began the day with the usual routine, preparing breakfast and expecting to see her husband home shortly from his night shift. He might have taken a ship to London, or perhaps undertaken local pilotage at Ramsgate or Whitstable. She would be glad to see his return for travelling conditions were again diabolical. Further snow was falling on icy roads, and it was 5 degrees below freezing.

The telephone interrupted Mrs Francis' thoughts. It was a pilot's wife who had already heard, unlike Mary, the dramatic news from Ramsgate.

"Are you OK?"

"I'm fine thanks. Not long to go now."

"Are you sure?"

"Yes, honestly. A check up next week, but no problems."

"But what about Jim? Is he OK?"

"Oh yes, he's fine too. Been on duty all night, should be home soon. But we're both fine thanks."

Mary put down the phone. How nice that people should be concerned over their welfare! After all, they had not been in the pilotage fraternity for long.

When Jim eventually arrived home later that morning, his wife took a long, hard look at his strange attire. "What on earth have you been up to?" Jim poured himself a stiff drink, told Mary to sit down, and described the interesting events of the night.

That might have been the end of the story, had it not been Jim Francis' determination to ensure that similar accidents could be avoided. He approached the Pilots' Committee, and a sub-committee was formed to approach the Board of Trade, through the United Kingdom Pilots Association, to change the rules on pilot ladder safety. His requests were met with a cool response, and when The Merchant Shipping (Pilot Ladders) Rules 1965 came into force that year, no mention was made to outlaw this killer equipment

Matters came to a head on 3rd August 1967 when the tragedy waiting to happen occurred off Dover. The British vessel *Afric* stopped off the port to land her Cinque Ports pilot, Jim Pearson. He had mounted the bulwark steps using the side rails for support as he turned with his back to the sea to begin his descent down the ladder. Whereupon, the whole apparatus tipped under his weight, and crashed down onto the boat below. The pilot landed in the water and according to the boatman, appeared to be swimming and then raising an arm as the boat drew near to him. That was the last movement that he was seen to make.

Further pressure on the Government minister failed to make any impression, and it was not until a meeting with local MP for Folkestone, Albert Costain, that the pilots felt they had found a sympathetic ear. He encouraged media attention, and a re-enactment of the incident with television coverage, and Jim Francis once again falling backwards into the water, this time from the relative safety of a ship in Dover docks. But it was not until 1970 that Albert Costain in a 10 minute Rule Bill in Parliament succeeded in changing the Board of Trade's reluctant attitude.

Looking back over the intervening years, it is clear that Jim Francis' dogged determination has since saved the lives of pilots, not only in the UK, but throughout the world. From that small beginning there are now in place strict regulations concerning ladders, clothing, launches and other aspects of pilots' safety.

Today that small ship leaving Ramsgate would have well lit access to the ladder, stanchions secured to the bulwark, and a crewman standing by with life-line and buoy. The pilot himself wears a reflective, inflatable jacket fitted with a powerful strobe light. The high-powered launch now has a two-man crew, a mechanical hoist at the stern, powerful searchlights, survival kit and VHF communication between ship, launch and Port control. No longer will that freezing body have to be lashed to the gunwale, and towed more dead than alive, back into harbour.

Chapter 12

Rendezvous

Rendezvous off Cherbourg with the Japanese *Sirius Highway* bound Sheerness. In bad weather with the possibility of launches being 'off station' at Folkestone, Ramsgate or the Sunk, expensive delays could be avoided by embarking the pilot by helicopter.

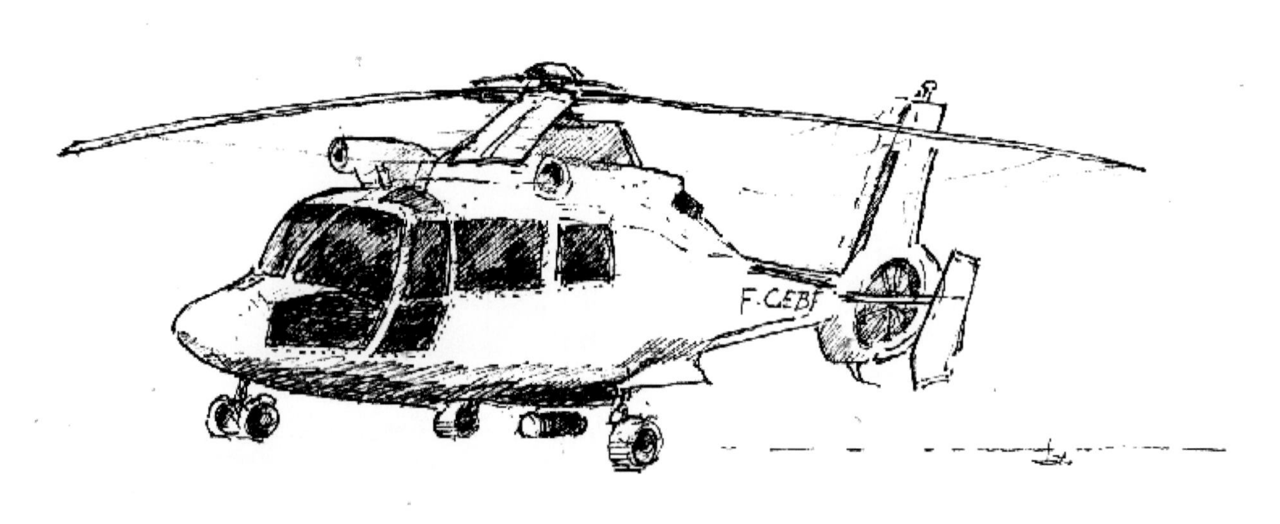

20/8/85. Rendezvous

Japanese "SIRIUS HIGHWAY" off Cherbourg
bound Sheerness

There are launches based at both Gravesend and Sheerness, but the busy pilot stations for entry to the Thames are situated at Harwich and Ramsgate that bear the brunt of the work and the weather. Harwich is the busier for this includes the heavy traffic using Felixstowe. Consequently there are three launches operational twenty-four hours a day, with a back up of four more in reserve. Five two-man crews provide continuity to each boat. With the rendezvous in the vicinity of the Sunk Light vessel involving a round trip of thirty miles, these craft have to be built to the highest specification. The 52 ft launches are fitted with Scania engines capable of 25 knots.

Ramsgate operates one boat, with two held in reserve. Sometimes during busy spells, as much as twenty hours of the twenty-four may be spent at sea. With an hour's round trip to the rendezvous near the North East spit buoy, it requires precise timing as inward and outward vessels pass their ETAs. Even with a procession of ships outward from London and the Medway, time must be found to return to base to pick up more pilots for inward ships without causing undue delay.

Without doubt the unsung heroes of the service are the boat crews to whom the pilot entrusts his safety. Theirs is an arduous job performed in all weathers, twenty-four hours a day throughout the year. Only when a gale builds up from a North to a S.E'ly quarter will the coxswain hesitate. He knows that big seas could damage his boat if he doesn't ease down on the throttles, especially at night when his searchlight is required to pick out the rogue waves. In such conditions he is aware of the mounting pressures - agents worrying whether their ship will be served and the huge cost of even a few hours delay - anxious captains pondering their next move as they approach the coast wondering whether the service is still in operation.

And the pilots themselves, outward bound in deteriorating weather and anxious not to be overcarried to the next port, can put the coxswain under further pressure. But it is the coxswain's decision, and if considers any risk exists, he will suspend the service. For while his launch could put to sea in any weather, it is at transfer where the danger lies. Though a large vessel provides a good lee, she might roll heavily with weather and swell abeam; the pilot ladder swinging clear one minute and crashing back against the ship's side the next, with perhaps the launch pinned against the listing ship as she comes alongside. The critical moment comes when the pilot, on his way down the ladder, reaches the bottom rungs. With the launch rising and falling several meters, it needs precise co-ordination between coxswain and pilot, before that leap backwards to the safety of the crewman standing by.

Before the change to Ramsgate, Margate pier used to be the base. In those days the messenger at the end of the pier, whilst keeping a radio watch, would also keep an eye open for incoming ships flying 'G' flag. But this was a very exposed mooring for the launch, and on one rough night the old *Nayland* broke adrift and was driven high and dry upon Margate beach.

Not long afterwards in 1978, a severe northerly storm shook Thanet, and totally destroyed the pier and lifeboat station. All that remained of Margate's prime attraction were the iron pilings, like so many headstones in some forgotten churchyard. After many complaints, the army were called in to blow them up. Gigantic explosions rent the air, some windows in the town were broken, but the pilings stood firm. And there they will remain until perhaps a more enterprising council can afford to rebuild the pier.

A busy night at the Sunk. The pilot cutter used to be stationed in the vicinity of the lightvessel until the introduction of the fast launches based at Harwich. Instead of 14 pilots onboard the cutter, the launch makes the fifteen mile transfer in forty minutes.

Bon Voyage!

Chapter Thirteen

VLCCs - Very Large Crude Carriers

Added variety to pilotage in the Thames is offered to those who undertake the berthing and unberthing of the large tankers at the refineries of Shellhaven*, Coryton and Canvey Island. This complex of jetties, situated ten miles west of Southend can accommodate anything from the small coastal tanker to the giant VLCC (Very Large Crude Carrier).

Oil was first imported to London's Victoria Dock in 1862, but fires and explosions occurred and it was felt prudent to look for a more suitable venue downstream and away from the highly populated areas. At that time Thameshaven had been a large importer of live cattle with rail communication direct to London, but when imports were prohibited in 1876, the first oil cargoes were landed here. Then in 1923, Cory Brothers of Cardiff decided to build a large refinery, and so Coryton was born.

By the late 1960s the size of the oil tanker suddenly increased tenfold. It was the birth of the VLCC with a length in excess of 300 metres and capacity of more than 300,000 tons. As far as the Thames is concerned the river is too shallow for these vessels when loaded, and they would have to be lightened in Europe before venturing into the river. In addition, dredging would be necessary to ensure such vessels remained afloat at their berths at low water.

Another problem the arrival of the VLCC brought to the surface was the revival of 'choice' pilotage which had existed since the earliest days when cutters from Dungeness, Hastings and as far as the Western Approaches would spend days searching down Channel for London bound ships and strike a price for pilotage.

Al Haramain at anchor near the Sunk light vessel awaiting the early flood before resuming passage to Coryton. Deadweight 284,000 tons, length 1120 ft, breadth 178 ft, Maximum draft 70 ft, TPI (Tons per inch immersion 405. Crash stop from full ahead: 2.8 miles in 24 minutes. It was a long haul from Folkestone to Thameshaven, and usually involved a staged anchoring to ensure arrival just before HW

Until the late 1980s many shipping companies had employed their own choice pilots for London and elsewhere, an arrangement that had become increasingly unpopular with the vast majority who did not have such a contract, but instead worked on an alphabetical roster awaiting their turn on the cutter stationed off Dungeness or Harwich. Here, long delays might well be experienced, with the last man waiting two, perhaps three days, especially if he was an under-draft pilot. In the meantime, the choice man jumped the queue, taking the train down to Brixham to join his passenger vessel bound for Tilbury. Of course, for the Master of such a ship, the choice system had great advantages. Here was a face he knew well, someone he could trust immediately, friends in common, with news of the other ships in the Company. But gradually, with the demise of the premier shipping companies, the choice system had become extinct until now, and pilots were not keen for it to be re-introduced. This was different. The oil companies wanted a 'specialist' used to handling these massive vessels. Common sense prevailed, agreement was reached, and at the beginning of the 1970s the Berthing service was formed. No longer would the estuary pilot, who may well have spent 12 hours on the bridge and much longer if joining at a continental port, be expected to berth the vessel as well. After such a passage, perhaps in adverse weather conditions, in heavy traffic, constant vigilance takes its toll and the prospect of the final manoeuvres, directing the tugs, swinging ship in the confined, shallow waters before berthing alongside a fragile jetty, could well have provided added stress.

The VLCC posed a series of problems. Instead of conning a conventional tanker of some 160 metres from a bridge amidships, here was a ship more than twice that length, twice the beam, ten times as heavy - and with the bridge aft. But the most worrying factor of such ships in the river is the draft. Frequent checks with the tidal gauges and comparison with the prediction tables are vital as the inward passage commences

Seven fairway buoys mark the centre-line of the narrow Sea Reach Channel which is ten miles long.
The oil refineries at Coryton and Shellhaven are in the distance

from the Sunk light vessel off Harwich at low water, carrying the rise of tide through the Black Deep, Knock John and Sea Reach channels. These large tankers, part discharged in Antifer, Lyme Bay or Rotterdam where drafts of 22 metres are common place, arrive off the shallow Thames estuary where the governing depth is a mere ten metres. Allowing for a rise of tide of five metres and a draft of perhaps fourteen metres, this leaves but one metre between the keel and the river bed. The margin is very fine. Other factors too, come into consideration. Unusual weather conditions will create a 'cut' in the tide necessitating an abort while there is still room to turn. 'Squat' will increase the draft of a large vessel in a narrow channel depending on her speed. So will the slightest list. Grounding could be fatal, with perhaps a broken back and the consequent pollution.

At a rendezvous at the end of the Sea Reach channel, it is the Berthing pilot's turn to take over the responsibility from the sea pilot. He clambers up the nine metre ladder from the tug and then the six decks up to the bridge. The fittest man can be somewhat breathless after such a climb, though one tries not to give that impression! At this point there are rather less than 5 miles to go before the swing off the berth, and as he eases the speed back from 7 knots, he has time enough to get the feel of the ship, secure his tugs and make sure the mooring arrangements are understood. With 'flags of convenience' now as commonplace as multi-national crews, the language barrier can pose a problem. Giving instructions to a Greek captain with very limited English who passes it on through his VHF radio to his Filipino crew at stations fore and aft tends to cause the occasional misunderstanding.

Tankers *Golden Crux No.8* and *Matco Thames* berthed at Coryton

Nowadays handling VLCCs in our restricted waters has been made easier with the advent of the highly manoeuvrable Voith tugs. When one is made fast aft, and pulling back at half power for twenty minutes, full control and steerage and steerage can be maintained with the tanker's main engine still turning ahead. Before the Voith appeared on the scene, astern movements would usually provoke a big 'cut' to starboard that could only be checked by the two powerful tugs fast forward, with a combined bollard pull of 100 tons, pulling hard on the port bow and thus inevitably increasing the headway. With the speed now down to 3 knots, not so easy to assess at night and 90 feet above the water, and carrying the last of the flood, now is the time for the turn. London Port control will have warned all ships that the manoeuvre will block the river for several minutes. Astern on the engine, and as the 30 feet diameter propeller bites, round go the tugs on the starboard beam, the stern tug to the port quarter, and a fourth ready to push up on the starboard side. Perhaps twenty minutes later, the swing is complete and the ship stationary off her berth, the mooring lines being run ashore by boat, and gently easing alongside the fragile jetty. Another job done, another safe arrival.

Now the majority of the Trinity House pilots have retired, and the new men spawned by the PLA have brought London into the 21st Century. New technology and new legislation has brought many changes and the job, unchanged for hundreds of years, will never be the same.

* Shellhaven closed down and dismantled (2001)

Chapter Fourteen

Margate Pier

Margate Pier played an important part in pilotage operations to and from the Thames estuary. Amongst the amusement stalls at the end of the pier, there was situated a small room manned by a messenger who monitored the two-way radio and VHF. His job was to co-ordinate the supply of pilots for inward ships, and their disembarkation from those outward bound. The rendezvous was the North-east Spit buoy four miles to the NE, the launch was on standby at the pier steps, and pilots immediately available.

Usually there were few problems, but there were times when the weather intervened to upset the best laid plans. A gale with a swell running would necessitate the launch taking shelter either at Margate's Stone Pier if there was sufficient water, or in Ramsgate round the coast five miles away, with pilots boarding and landing there. Further deterioration of conditions placed the responsibility squarely on the coxswain. Should he decide to go 'Off Station' then serious disruption to shipping was unavoidable.

The Master of an inward ship would have been in contact with the pilot station, confirming his ETA, draft and destination. Worsening conditions as he approached the coast his first concern. Lights from anchored vessels in Margate Roads, fishing vessels difficult to pick up until at close range. He would have been glad to welcome the pilot onboard, until the VHF radio splutters into life. "All ships, all ships, NE Spit Pilotage suspended until weather improves."

The messenger's job could become a nightmare on those busy occasions of heavy outward and inward traffic. Some launches were slower than others, and with the old *Reculver* on service, 12 knots was a modest speed to service perhaps half a dozen ships at a time.

The Day After. The NNE Storm has done its worst. The Lifeboat House in the middle distance collapsed into the sea soon afterwards.

On 11th January, 1978, a storm of unprecedented violence was to change everything. For some years the pier had been declared unsafe and the gates locked. Only the pilot messenger in his lonely vigil 400 yards out into the North Sea remained with his launch crew to keep him company. Pilots and lifeboat crew were issued keys to the pier. The forecast that night was for strengthening Northerly winds. Already the launch was ranging uneasily in the increasing swell. It was time to head for Ramsgate and the safety of an enclosed harbour.

But within minutes the seas were transformed into seething white breakers as the wind increased from force 6 to hurricane force 12 from the NNE. Many events happened almost simultaneously, but the first casualty was the pilot launch whose moorings were snapped like cotton as she was driven ashore on Margate beach. There was just time for the messenger and crew to beat a hasty retreat from the pier as the boiling waves surged below and about them.

Much damage was sustained along the Thanet coastline that night, but the saddest sight of all was to witness the gradual disintegration of that much-loved landmark. By morning the buildings at the end of the pier had been completely destroyed, and the lifeboat house situated halfway along the pier reduced to matchwood. Thousands watched as the heavy swell and mountainous seas did their work. The coastline was littered with the wreckage. Great bulks of timber that had formed the framework of the pier were tossed ashore like matchsticks. By afternoon only a skeleton remained, with the end of the pier an island on its own. It was the end of an era for the people of Thanet.

For many years Margate has boasted an extremely efficient lifeboat service with a proud record of many lives saved and ships assisted. Within minutes of the warning rockets, the crew would be onboard, boat house doors opened, engine started and the coxswain ready to release the lifeboat down the steep slipway.

Stone Pier, with the remains of the old pier in the distance

Paddle steamer *Waverley* embarking passengers from Stone Pier at HW

Post 1978 the RNLI had no option but to resort to a tractor launching for the Mersey Class boat. It is a 300 yard tow from the new lifeboat station, and considerably more if its low tide.
One winter's night I boarded a small ship off the North Foreland. Northeasterly weather and a big swell running. At the red flashing East Margate buoy, course was set for the Princes Channel en route for London, with the wind abeam, vessel rolling heavily, and the treacherous Margate Sands, a lee shore to port. Not an unusual situation - the visibility was good even though the conditions were uncomfortable. But I was soon to be reminded that only constant vigilance will achieve safety. Unknown to me, the ship was loaded with steel coils causing the magnetic compass to register an error of 30 degrees. I had not double checked our course made good and it was not until the vessel was surrounded by white, seething foam that I realised we were about to go ashore on the Margate Sands. Starboard, and more starboard, and slowly, reluctantly, the vessel clawed away from danger. A very close call, and a situation for which I alone was responsible. Had the ship stranded, possibly lost and within sight of my home, there would have followed a visit to Trinity House, a six months 'holiday' or perhaps worse.

Margate panorama, with Stone pier, the Big Wheel and Arlington House on the right

Chapter Fifteen

Around the North Foreland

North Foreland

Situated on the chalk cliffs of Northeast Kent, North Foreland Lighthouse commands a magnificent view over the Dover Straits, the southern North Sea and the Thames estuary. Its white flashing light (5 every 20 seconds) beckons the mariner from as far as 25 miles distant, whilst its red sector warns of the proximity of the treacherous Margate Sands. Coming up from the South in a small ship bound London, it makes a change to close the cliffs to half a mile, up to the Longnose Buoy off Cliftonville, then to bear away due west past Margate and the North Kent coast via the Horse and Gore Channel.

Once clear of the North Foreland, the Thames estuary stretches out before you, and clearly visible ahead were the Tongue Sands Towers with the Tongue Light Vessel on station 1.5 miles NNE. Unfortunately both these marks have long since disappeared, the former due to stress of weather though not before the two anti-aircraft guns had been salvaged, and the light vessel replaced by a buoy. In fog these had provided very reassuring targets on the radar screen, as they marked the entrances to the Princes and Edinburgh Channels. There is a choice of route here depending upon the size and draft of vessel, and the state of tide. A coaster of 1000 grt, draft 12 ft, and a flooding tide, might decide on the short cut, following the North Kent coast and through the Horse and Gore Channel. With only 4 foot of water at LWS, this course requires careful timing for the sake of only 20 minutes. We called it the ‘overland route’.

At the other end of the scale, there is no such option for the deep draft container ship, bulker or VLCC bound for the Thames. Such vessels, drawing as much as 14 metres or more, continue north past the Kentish Knock to the Longsand Head Buoy (near the Sunk Lightvessel), before making the big turn to the SW into the Black Deep. (NB. Entry to this channel is now at No. 8 Black Deep Buoy, Fishermen’s Gat.)

Vessels of intermediate size and draft would have the option of either the Princes or Edinburgh Channels. Over the years the latter has silted considerably and the buoys marking it withdrawn. Long gone are the days when the North Edinburgh, though narrow, was 10 metres at Low Water Springs, and the only route for deep draft ships. The neighbouring South Edinburgh Channel was only slightly shallower, and offered an alternative in heavy traffic conditions. Now that the Princes Channel has been dredged it is a straight forward entry into the Thames compared with the tortuous S bends of the Edinburgh Channels across which both the flood and ebb tide run strongly.

When not working, my hobby took me to the other side of the lighthouse, the golf course! The views here too are magnificent, with every tee and green affording a panorama of the sea, lighthouse, and all too frequently the pilot boat appearing out of the corner of the eye! More than once I have been lining up a putt, using the distant horizon as a spirit level when the launch would come clear of a line of trees to disturb my concentration! In 1998 North Foreland was the last lighthouse in the UK to become fully automated.

Thanet is renowned for its magnificent beaches, and the numerous sheltered bays gouged into the chalk cliffs such as Botany, Joss, and Kingsgate that are great favourites. Great favourites too for the wrecking gangs of centuries past, who, having lured a ship onto a lee shore with flares from a cliff top, would manhandle the cargoes into the many tunnels hewn into the cliffs and thence into the cellars of 'safe' houses. John Buchan based the title of *The Thirty-Nine Steps* on one such cliff-top house at Stone Gap in Broadstairs. Nor was he alone among Thanet's celebrities. Charles Dickens was inspired as he wrote at his desk overlooking the harbour at

Broadstairs, as was J M W Turner at his easel overlooking Margate with uninterrupted views of both sunrise and sunset over the sea. Sadly the house where he boarded has been demolished, but lottery money has been granted for the Turner Centre to be built at the harbour. Vincent Van Gogh taught art in Ramsgate, and Walter Sickert lived and worked in St Peters, Broadstairs.

The demise of Margate was hastened when the pier was destroyed in 1978. Long gone are the heady days of trips from London in the *Royal Daffodil.* The Lido with its large swimming pool has long since been filled in. No more the long waiting lists for a beach hut site, for now they would all be vandalized. Instead it is the ubiquitous jet skis with the attendant cars and trailers that crowd the promenades and beaches. The coastguard station situated on the most strategic site in Britain, with views encompassing the Thames estuary, Dover Straits and the Goodwins is no longer manned. Even the sewage pumping station at Foreness Point, which had operated efficiently since the 1920s by means of a lunar clock ensuring the release of sewage on the ebb tide directly away from the coast, has suffered 'improvements'. The sewage outfall pipes were lengthened to enable the discharge of screened raw sewage at any time of the tide. Consequently during flood tides and onshore winds the beaches become polluted. What price progress?

The quarantine anchorage off Margate can become quite congested at times with vessels awaiting berths, clearance, orders or sheltering from heavy weather. But when a gale blows from the north, despite the good holding ground, it is as well move well clear of the lee shore and re-anchor or just heave-to further out to sea. One vessel which did not heed the warnings was the Greek bulk carrier, *Argos* 12000 tons, awaiting orders having discharged her sugar cargo in the Thames at Silvertown.

Reflections   Kingsgate Bay, Broadstairs

The wind which had been in the north-east for weeks, increased to gale force and the *Argos* began dragging towards the shore. Due to windlass failure, efforts to weigh anchor were unsuccessful, and despite astern and ahead movements on the main engine, the vessel grounded on the hard sand and rock of Margate beach on a receding tide and heavy surf, heading Southwest.

With no change in the weather forecast it might have taken 4 tugs at High Water to pull her off had it been possible to put tow lines onboard. A large deep sea tug *Far Turbot* was by chance only 300 meters away and most anxious to take a line, a task which would not have been impossible, given the help of the Ramsgate lifeboat (coxswain Ron Cannon) which stood by, wallowing in the surf surrounding the stricken ship.

Argos, 12000 grt Greek bulk carrier, ashore on Margate Sands 1996

By all accounts this immediate help was refused as the Captain had already called out the possibly cheaper tugs from Dover. Unbelievably, in mid-afternoon, with the tide still low and without assistance, *Argos,* with engine thrashing astern, came clear of the lee-shore and re-anchored several miles off, having suffered no apparent damage. The Captain would have had to make out a grounding report and perhaps receive a reprimand from his owners, but a salvage claim from a tug once made fast would have cost millions: a very close call indeed.

Tongue Sands Tower complete with anti-aircraft guns

Until the mid-1990s, the approaches to the Princes Channel were clearly defined by one of the WW2 forts strategically positioned throughout the estuary. The Tongue Sands Fort, listing heavily for years, finally slid beneath the surface and is now marked by a pair of Cardinal buoys. But what a story these forts have to tell, for they played no small part in the defence of London. They were credited with 22 enemy aircraft shot down, one E-boat sunk, and 20 to 30 flying bombs destroyed, as well as many rescue operations for ditched airmen. In February 1942, the first of the massive structures, Rough's Fort, as large as the *Arc de Triomphe*, displacing 4500 tons, was towed from its Gravesend dockyard by 3 large tugs to a final resting place off Felixstowe. Great care was required to sink the massive 168 by 88 feet concrete pontoon bearing in mind that the fort was fully loaded with stores, heavy ammunition and 120 men. Once the tow was in position, the 12" valve was opened, and taking 15 minutes for the pontoon to flood, there followed a rapid 15 second descent for the bow to strike the sea bed, followed 30 seconds by the grounding of the stern. At the moment the bow hit the sea bed, the fort was at an angle of 30 degrees, a most uncomfortable moment for those onboard.

Within the year three more forts had been built and positioned in the estuary, Sunk Head, Knock John and the Tongue Sands. And soon afterwards 3 more forts of different design were established at the Nore, Red Sands and Shivering Sands. The forts fared with less distinction after the war. In the 1950s a Swedish ship knocked over one of the towers in the Nore group, which made it a danger to navigation. The damaged fort was dismantled. Shivering Sands too suffered collision from an outward bound ship in fog. Part of one of the towers lodged on the vessel's fore deck, and an unscheduled call at Ramsgate was required to remove the offending deck cargo! Meanwhile the Sunk Head tower was blown up, and the Knock John rendered inaccessible. In the 1960s pirate radio broadcasting came into vogue, and in quick succession the Shivering Sands fort was occupied by Radio City, Red Sands fort by Radio 390 and the Knock John by entrepreneur Roy Bates before he took over the Roughs Tower.

Chapter Sixteen

Lynne Ennis

One of the characters to be found on the waterfront was Cecil 'Bill' Ennis. He had been a 'Freeman of the River' for many years, and was a pilot with a difference. Not licensed by Trinity House for the river, but with a 'gentlemen's agreement' with Agents, Owners and Captains to manoeuvre their ships within the numerous systems of enclosed locks, for which in fact, no license was required at all. The job was usually handed down through the generations of families, and offered little security, for with only verbal agreement there was nothing to stop interference from outsiders who might offer a cut price service.

However, Bill's specialised services were much sought after, and on occasion he would find himself in demand in quick succession either in the King George V Docks, Royal Albert and Victoria complex, Millwall and West India, Surrey Commercial, London or Tilbury Docks.

Within the confines of an enclosed dock there is little room for error. The columns of berthed ships being very vulnerable as they worked their cargoes usually with shore cranes on the one side, and with ships' derricks into lighters on the other. Loose barges, floating cranes and other ships on the move added to the hazards. In his early years on the bridge, Bill would have had to communicate by whistle with the tugs made fast fore and aft, but the advent of portable VHF radio made life much easier, with more precise information immediately available.

The Master of a ship, having just crossed an ocean where by careful celestial navigation he would have established his position within 3 miles, felt completely helpless as a complete stranger negotiated his beloved vessel through locks with but inches to spare, passing stern first through the narrow cutting and swing bridge between Royal Albert and King George V Docks, and then backing down the length of the dock between columns of ships.

Over the centuries, licensed watermen had been much in demand from sculling passengers across the river, tending moorings, towing barges, but in more recent years their expertise was restricted to the enclosed docks, and there were soon not enough jobs to go round. But Bill Ennis had that secret ingredient which every successful pilot enjoys: the confidence of the Captain. In such close quarter situations, the most competent shipmaster might well become nervous, but he will be less inclined to question and interfere if he has full trust in his pilot.

Bill Ennis had a young daughter, Lynne, who loved the river. Every spare moment was spent afloat on the Thames or accompanying her father as he plied his trade. Perhaps one day I'll be a dock pilot too, she told herself. Though for a woman to imagine herself capable of such a job was unthinkable. Her apprenticeship for 'Freeman of the River' commenced when she was 18, and then although having twice failed her 'Twos' exam, she started her training as a dock pilot with Bill two years later. After a further three years Lynne had done sufficient time to sit for the passing out exam for 'Freeman of the River'. With her father's blessing she presented herself at the elegant Waterman's Hall, St Mary's-at-Hill

Lynne sat before a committee of 10, chaired by the Master of the Waterman's Company. She fought hard to keep her composure, knowing full well that there were some she faced across the semi-circular desk who would be keen to see her fail. 'Knowledge of the River' was a very thorough examination covering depths, tidal effects, location of berths and 'stairs', heights of the working arches at bridges, manoeuvring with models, signals, knots and much else. After a grilling lasting an hour and a half, it was all over. Had she done well enough to pass? Was she about to become the first female dock pilot on the river Thames?

Manoeuvring a bulk carrier into Tilbury lock.
Once inside, the dock pilot would take over

Would the Equal Opportunities Bill for Women that became law in 1978 work in her favour? Lynne was soon to know the answer. “Your knowledge was not up to the required standard, come back in 6 months if you wish to re-sit the examination.”

Though disappointed, Lynne knew of other candidates who failed first time, so back she went to work, learning from her father’s expertise and revising her ‘Knowledge’. Six months passed, and feeling more confident, she presented herself at Waterman’s Hall. The questions were answered without difficulty. Once again she waited outside, but once again she was to learn of her failure, and yet again 6 months later.

Despite these setbacks, the Owners, Captains and Agents held Bill Ennis in such high regard that they were more than happy to employ his daughter even though she had not yet passed her ‘Freeman of the River’. Bill decided that his daughter was ‘ready’ in September 1986, when he told her that she’d have to manage on her own as he was off on a fortnight’s holiday. In truth it would not be her first time ‘solo’. That moment had already passed a week before...

A large Brazilian ship *Lloyd Bahia* had entered Tilbury lock and was to be moved to her berth as soon as the gates opened. Bill Ennis was an old friend of Captain Roberto, and after a quiet word with him, they both went down to breakfast. Meanwhile Lynne had taken charge of the manoeuvre, confident in the knowledge that her father was on the opposite bridge wing, 100 foot away, and in VHF communication should she need advice... The ‘job’ went well, tugs, engine movements and the intricate manoeuvre backing the ship up to her berth. On completion she walked into the wheelhouse to have her bill signed. “The Captain is below having breakfast with your father,” said the Chief Officer.

Small container vessel *Carrybox 4* inward bound in Gravesend Reach

After yet another failure at Waterman's Hall, Lynne almost gave up in despair, but the death of her father in February 1987 redoubled her determination to follow in his footsteps, though there were moves afoot by rivals to take over Bill's work at Tilbury now that the other enclosed docks up river had closed down. The next month, Lynne undertook an act of pilotage that was to shake her confidence, and one that she would not have attempted had she been more experienced.

On a day of severe gales, the large 30,000 ton China Ocean Shipping Co *Shahe* had been manoeuvred with difficulty into the lock from the river prior to her final negotiation to No. 45 Berth. Four tugs were ordered to assist swing the vessel to starboard after clearing the lock before backing up to her berth half a mile astern.

Lynne considered her options. If she delayed it would upset the programme of the other vessels. If she proceeded, she was well aware that the swing to starboard would bring the full force of the westerly gale on to the beam. *Shahe* had a big freeboard, and with containers 4 high on deck, she would set to leeward quickly in the enclosed space. Her worst fears were realised as she ordered the forward tugs to bring the bows round with the ship's engines going astern. With the gale now on the starboard beam, and all tugs on full power, the ship set down heavily on to the knuckle (the right angle between No. 1 and 36 Berth). Holed above the waterline, but at least they were alongside even if it was the wrong berth. The Chinese Captain was tearing his hair out, but luckily could speak no English!

When leaving Tilbury Lock in a large ship with the flood tide on the port bow, it is risky to turn that way without coming close to the south shore. The safe option is a complete swing to starboard.

When the weather abated the next day, Lynne completed the job, and the vessel repaired within a further two days. Despite this misfortune, another failure of her Waterman's exam and further mutterings about whether she was suited to the job, Lynne finally passed at her fifth attempt in December 1987. Bill's faith in his daughter was justified. Lynne belief in herself and her dogged determination won through. Her expertise is now as much sought after as was her father's.

Chapter Seventeen

'Nightmare' *Monte Ulia*

For most seafarers looking back over their careers, the years have passed without undue incident - just fading memories of distant lands, long ocean passages and those few precious days of home leave in between. Perhaps that first voyage serving under a 'Captain Bligh' is best forgotten. On the other hand, exotic lands on the other side of the globe, those tropical nights out on deck in a hammock, gathering flying fish off the decks at daybreak, days of unbroken sunshine and multicoloured sunsets, all provide ample compensation.

For a few, amongst those fading memories, there are moments so vivid, so indelibly imprinted that it might have been only yesterday - one unforgettable moment. A moment perhaps when a decision has to be made, without second thought, to avert disaster. It is that moment of truth which only happens to other people one reads about in the news headlines. The reaction when confronted by a burglar in one's own home; the reaction to a puncture in the fast lane; or the reaction to an imminent collision with another ship.

It is fortunate for most of us that such decisions do not have to be made. The thought of cracking a burglar's skull with a golf club while reaching for the phone as you place a foot upon his twitching body may fill one with satisfaction and pride. In reality one's reaction cannot be measured unless or until that dreaded moment arrives. That moment of truth!

Rounding the South Foreland inward bound

The reactions on the bridge of White Star's *Titanic* to the lookouts' warning were immediate, but it was already too late. There was no time either, for the fully laden tanker *Torrey Canyon*. Having taken a short cut, her moment of truth was on a time fuse. At full speed the bottom was ripped out of the ship on the Seven Stones reef, disgorging 117,000 tons of crude oil into the sea. Sometimes that moment extends itself into hours. When the *Amoco Cadiz*, another fully laden supertanker developed steering failure on a lee shore off Brittany, there was yet time enough to avert the most horrendous oil spillage and shipwreck, but by the time permission had been granted by the Chicago head office to accept a tow, several hours had passed. By then it was too late.

* * *

By the very nature of his work, the 'moment of truth' for a pilot is never far away. Heavy traffic, close quarter situations, thick fog, strong tides and shallow water are constant companions, though he would not survive long were he to worry about what *could* happen. But whatever the conditions, the depth of water remains the overriding consideration. There are few areas in the Thames estuary that a deep draft vessel will remain afloat at low water. Such a vessel must use the rising tide to negotiate the shallows, and be secured in her dredged berth before the tide falls away. Outward bound, perhaps on a falling tide, it is even more critical as these same shallows must be crossed while there is still enough water.

But rarely, if ever in the Thames, have the ingredients for disaster for disaster been mixed together into one powerful cocktail. Collision, fire, grounding and pollution, with a passenger vessel playing the central role.

26 July, 1970, and at Folkestone a beautiful summer evening. The Duty Pilot in the Ops room overlooking the harbour, had just recorded a tape of ETAs for London and ports in the Thames estuary. Pilots on the roster were thus able to phone in and establish roughly when they could expect a call and for what ship: whether to have an early night at home, or come to base to be on hand. A great improvement on the old days, pre 1967, when 14 pilots were afloat in the cutter off Dungeness whether there were ships due or not.

Trinity House v/s *Siren* replenishing the Tongue Lightvessel off Margate

Until the lightvessels became automated or replaced by buoys, they were manned by a crew of four working month on, month off. With time on their hands, favourite past-times were fishing, tapestry, model making and painting. Not so comfortable in rough weather, or when the foghorn was sounding off twenty feet above your head!

There was a busy programme that night. Apart from the London-bound ETAs, there was a tanker for Canvey Island, three vessels for the Medway, two for Dover and a coaster bound Whitstable. Dover was always a popular choice for it was only a 6 mile run which paid a full 'sharing turn' from the Common Purse equal to the next pilot who might have to take his deep draft ship the long way round, 100 miles via the Black Deep off Harwich. To add insult to injury, the Dover-bound pilot would also receive mooring fees in the enclosed docks which were outside the London District and thus non-sharing. Whitstable ships on the other hand were to be avoided whenever possible. Such vessels were few and far between, and consequently a pilot's knowledge of the harbour and approaches somewhat limited. At night the town's lights obscure the leading lights, and with the tide running across the narrow entrance, it provided a stern test for the most competent pilot.

The job of the night was undoubtedly the Spanish passenger vessel *Monte Ulia* inward bound for Tilbury after her round trip to the Canaries. Her pilot was ready and waiting and pleased at the prospect of a pleasant run up river, and back home by the early hours.

At 20 knots, powered by twin Perkins diesels, the launch cleared the harbour in a lazy arc for the rendezvous one and a half miles from the breakwater. Soon after 7 pm John Natcott-West had arrived on *Monte Ulia*'s bridge to the customary warm welcome from her Captain, and a steward with the dinner menu in the background. Course was set, dinner ordered and by the time the ship had negotiated the ferry traffic off Dover, John had settled down to his meal in the wheelhouse and the Captain had gone below to join his table. Round the South Foreland and St Margaret's Bay, course was set for the Downs, the route inside the Goodwins. The sun was low over the cliffs, visibility was excellent and little traffic to worry about apart from some yachts catching the dying breeze and fishing boats returning to Ramsgate.

Monte Ulia, one of the Aznar fleet was 8000 grt, 143m in length, with a crew of 83. Also onboard were 163 passengers many of whom strolled the decks enjoying the balmy evening. Soon after passing Ramsgate, the North Foreland lighthouse came abeam three miles distant, and beyond Thanet the lurid colours of a brilliant sunset, as brilliant as those which inspired Turner during his years at Margate. It is at times like this that a pilot feels he would do the work for nothing, and makes up for those trips on a small coaster rolling heavily in a NE'ly gale off the Foreland at 3 o'clock on a freezing morning, holding onto the binnacle for dear life...

Soon after 9 pm *Monte Ulia* entered the Princes Channel, and the ebb tide reduced her manoeuvring speed from 14 to 12 knots. Radio contact was made with Gravesend, giving ETA 0030 and draft 7 meters. Shivering Sands Towers were soon visible in the gathering dusk, fine to starboard. Then the Red Sands Towers to port, and then at 10.30pm the Sea Reach Channel. Exactly one hour remained.

At the same time, twenty miles upstream, the motor barge *Banco,* 500grt and 51m in length, had left her berth in Gravesend on a routine passage to load fuel at Coryton. She was scheduled to arrive there at 11.30 pm.

The main jetty, Coryton No. 4 had just been completed to accommodate the new breed of supertanker, the VLCC (Very Large Crude Carrier) of 300,000 tons deadweight and 350m in length. The causeway to the jetty head was 1500ft long, wide enough for vehicle access and supporting a 36" diameter crude oil discharge pipeline. The jetty head itself was 120 ft long and equipped with 4 massive 16" control booms and one 12" fuel boom, all capable of reaching over a VLCC in ballast. A large 6 storey control house was situated next to the booms, surmounted by a crane for handling gangways and ships stores. High level fire-fighting monitors were stationed on the building for directing both at flow booms and vessel alongside. The new super jetty had taken years to construct and cost many millions. Opposite the jetty is positioned the Mid Blythe Buoy which marks the southern edge of the deep water channel, three and a half cables in width.

Tug outward bound in the Sea Reach - with a following breeze

At 11.18 pm *Monte Ulia* passed No. 7, the last of the Sea Reach Buoys, and course was set to pass between the Coryton jetties and the Mid Blythe. By now it was dark, visibility good, no reports of tanker movements apart from the *Esso Nordica* at London & Coastal Oil Jetty which had tugs in attendance prior to her departure. Neither was there any inward traffic. Only *Banco* outward bound and approaching Mid Blythe 2.5 miles away. In all probability the two vessels would pass each other off Coryton. It was unusually quiet, and the fairway clear of fishing boats and other craft. As passing vessels approach each other, it is always reassuring to see the other's red side light, thus confirming what the aspect of her masthead lights have already indicated. In this area, it is customary to see the green light of an outward vessel until she bears away 10 degrees to starboard rounding the Mid Blythe buoy.

. John Natcott-West watched carefully the masthead lights and green side light fine on his port bow. At a distance of a mile he altered 5 degrees to starboard to allow more room for this small vessel. Surely now those mast lights would come into line and then the red light appear. It is a situation in which a pilot frequently finds himself, and is resolved when the target vessel settles onto the new course and passes clear, red to red.

Moments later, it became apparent that more evasive action would be necessary. The vessels were closing rapidly. 'Starboard more. One short blast'. But even as *Monte Ulia* swung so did the other vessel swing to port across the river and thus maintaining the same aspect, fine on the port bow.

By now only 1.5 cables (900ft) separated them, *Banco* athwart the river, and *Monte Ulia* swinging past NW. But now in order to avoid collision, it was "Hard Astarboard. Full Astern, and a series of short blasts on the whistle." It was the moment of truth, the moment to wake up, sweating, from a nightmare.

VLCC at No. 4 Coryton jetty which *Monte Ulia* destroyed.

The Captain hurried to the bridge, too late to witness the collision avoidance. But by now the towering oil jetty lay dead ahead and despite the emergency astern revolutions, this collision could not be avoided. General Emergency stations was sounded on the whistle and internal alarms.

At 11.30 pm *Monte Ulia,* still swinging under the influence of the helm and transverse thrust of her propeller, smashed into the head of No. 4 Coryton oil jetty. Incredibly the force of the ship cut a swathe through the heavy concrete structure mounted on steel piling driven deep into the river bed, demolishing the control tower and the bank of flow booms some of which fell across her decks

All the massive pipelines were ruptured spilling a deadly cocktail of 400 tons of crude oil, fuel oil and gas oil into the river. Sparks showered the night sky from the short circuited and earthed power cables. The spilled oil quickly ignited, and flames silhouetted the stricken vessel.

But *Monte Ulia* had not yet finished her path of destruction. Engines still thrashing astern, she was through the wreckage of the jetty and now being carried by the ebb through the causeway connecting the jetty head with the refinery ashore. More ruptured fuel lines fuelled the fires surrounding the ship. Once clear of the causeway, despite efforts to swing into deeper water, *Monte Ulia* finally grounded on Holehaven Spit.

After the noise of grinding steel, smashing concrete, whistle signals, alarm bells and thudding engines, all was now strangely quiet. Burning oil surrounded the ship. It was a like scene from hell.

Within half a mile of the carnage, the two large tugs *Sun XXV1* and *Moorcock* assisting the departure of *Esso Nordica*, were released, and made full speed to the scene. Each tug was fitted with powerful fire-fighting equipment. Despite the dangerous ebb tide, they rounded the wreckage of the jetty, and passed through the gap created in the causeway, directing their foam nozzles at the burning oil surrounding the ship and onto the oil pulsing into the river from the fractured pipelines. Meanwhile the Emergency services had been alerted, and a full scale operation was soon under way.

With the burning wreckage of No 4 Coryton in the background, *Monte Ulia* severs the pipeline and causeway before grounding on Holehaven Spit. (Impression)

Gradually the fires were brought under control, isolated and extinguished as they drifted downstream. The tugs also managed to douse the blazing fires on a pontoon and a lighter before they drifted down onto the tankers and oil complex of nearby Canvey Island. With *Monte Ulia* now safe from fire, the tugs were able to return to the burning wreckage of No. 4 Jetty.

In 1878 the paddle steamer *Princess Alice* was in collision with the collier *Bywell Castle* under pilotage in Galleons Reach. With bodies being recovered from the river for weeks afterwards, the final tally was 640 dead. Here at Coryton not a soul was even slightly injured, but what might so easily have been... Perhaps 246 passengers and crew burned alive or drowned as they jumped overboard. Perhaps burning oil setting other jetties and vessels on fire downstream. To suffer collision, fire and grounding in the space of minutes could only happen in a nightmare. And yet another Thames tragedy so very nearly occurred on that clear summer night in 1970.

At 4.20 the following morning, *Monte Ulia* was refloated, and though badly damaged, proceeded under her own power, assisted by *Sun XXVI* on the last few miles of her voyage to Tilbury.

Chapter Eighteen

Stefan Batory: A night to remember

It is not often that the British climate rates the headlines. It is usually predictable, and more often than not brought upon the wings of depressions from the Atlantic. On the evening of 15th October 1987, yet another depression was working its way into the Western Approaches, and from this was spawned another intense depression which gathered power as it crossed into northern France. A storm of hurricane proportions was winding itself up for an assault on southern England, and no-one, certainly not Michael Fish at the Met. Office, was prepared for its ferocity when it crossed the coast in the early hours of next morning. All but the heaviest sleeper awoke to the howl of the wind shrieking in from the south. Gusts well in excess of 100 mph were recorded, and it was as well that the storm did not strike in daylight for the number of deaths and injuries would have been multiplied. Damage ran into millions of pounds. Roofs ripped from buildings, chimneys and walls down. Lorries, buses, caravans and cars were thrown about like so much matchwood. Bur above all, the damage to, and by trees. The preceding weeks of considerable rainfall had softened the ground, nor had the trees yet lost their leaves. Consequently the high resistance above, coupled with their weakened roots, caused millions to fall onto roads, railways, buildings, power cables and telephone lines.

The news bulletins bore grim tidings as the first streaks of daylight crossed the sky and the wind eased to a mere strong gale. There were reports of fatal accidents, closed roads, railways and schools, power cuts and further untold damage. Except for the severely restricted public services, few people ventured from their homes that day. In such weather conditions, it is arguably safer to be at sea in a well-found ship with plenty of sea room, than to be huddled under the bedclothes wondering if the chimney is going to crash through the roof or whether the windows are about to be blown in.

Such thoughts did not enter the mind of Peter Lloyd-Jones as he drove to Folkestone that evening before the Great Storm. He was the Trinity House pilot ‘on turn’, and had received orders to board the large Polish passenger ship *Stefan Batory* inward bound from Montreal, and to conduct her round the Kent coast and through the Thames estuary to Tilbury. Peter announced himself over the intercom at the main entrance of the pilot station. The lift whisked him up to the control room at the top of the tower, where the Duty pilot sat with his assistant. They discussed the job briefly. "Miserable evening, all night job, but a good fast ship, no delays, and berth on arrival."

This was much preferable to a low powered coaster of 8 knots that might have taken twelve uncomfortable hours to reach her destination. It was difficult to see much through the control room windows with the reflection of lights and the rain slanting across the glass, but the duty pilot checked the radar and picked up a large echo rounding Dungeness twelve miles distant. Moments later came VHF confirmation from the ship itself. "We are half an hour from the rendezvous."

Peter relaxed in an easy chair below until the phone rang from up top. "Four miles, have a good trip." This was his signal to move for the short walk down to the harbour, and the climb down the iron runged ladder to the waiting launch. It was calm enough in the harbour, but once clear of the breakwater, the coxswain had to ease back on the powerful twin engines, and to use his searchlight to pick up the crests and troughs of heavy seas. As the two vessels neared each other, one and a half miles south of the pierhead, *Stefan Batory* eased her speed and altered course to bring the wind abeam and a lee as the launch came alongside beneath the ladder. It was not a long climb for there was an opening halfway up the ship's side. Peter was greeted by the junior OOW, who led the way through the numerous passageways and staircases. There were the distant sounds of dance music as passengers savoured their last night of entertainment, while others were busy packing in readiness for the morning's disembarkation.

Folkestone Pilot Station

In the inky blackness of the bridge, Peter introduced himself to the Captain. They exchanged the usual pleasantries - good voyage, lousy night, and the more relevant details concerning the ship's draft of 8 meters and speed of 16 knots. "Steer 070 please and full speed. We have a ready berth at Tilbury stage. Let's see, 2315 now, 76 miles to go, this wind will hold her back. Should be there by 0500." Once settled on course, though the lights of Folkestone were clear enough abeam, he checked the radar to confirm the Dover breakwater to port, six miles distant. And so began an act of pilotage which Peter had performed many hundreds of times before, but one that would remain etched forever in his memory.

It was quiet up there on the bridge 80 feet above the water line. Just the clicking of the gyro compass, the steady drone of the radar, and the window wipers moving from side to side. There was occasional chatter from the VHF, Dover Port control talking to ferries as they approached or left the harbour. This was a particularly busy and potentially dangerous area. Vessels bound London invariably found Dover bound ferries on their starboard bow. Such circumstances required an early course alteration, and in restricted visibility radar plotting and VHF communication was an added insurance. Even as *Stefan Batory* was passing Dover, one of the many tragedies to occur that night was being spawned off Dungeness where the British coaster *Sumnia* had developed engine trouble and was drifting helplessly in a NE'ly direction towards Dover. Hours later she was to strike the western pier head and break up with the loss of two crew.

Once clear of Dover there is an option of routes, either inside or outside the Goodwins. There is a well-buoyed channel inside called The Downs which is limited in depth to only eight meters, but which is three miles shorter. Under the circumstances, with the following wind making steering more difficult, it was more prudent to skirt the Goodwins leaving the three light vessels to port. Rounding the North Foreland with its powerful light piercing the black night five times every 20 seconds, *Stefan Batory* set course NW for the narrow, s-shaped Edinburgh Channel where there would be only a meter and a half under the keel. The gale was now increasing from the south, and for the first time *Stefan Batory* felt the power of the wind as she listed gently to starboard. Steering was now becoming more difficult, starboard helm required to maintain course, and with a big starboard turn coming up at the entrance to the Edinburgh. Not long after LW, Peter was aware that the shallow water would further affect the steering. He spoke for the first time with TNS (Thames Navigation Service) on VHF.

"Approaching the Edinburgh channel inward bound. Anything outward?"

"No, you have a clear run and ready berth at Tilbury stage."

"We have a strong southerly gale here. What strength have you at Gravesend?"

"Wind here still 20 knots," was the reply.

Lloyd-Jones stood in the centre of the darkened wheelhouse in front of the Polish helmsman, the reflected glow from the compass illuminating his face as he steadied the ship upon each new course. Starboard to North, then easy round to the WSW at each pair of buoys. It was 2 o'clock. Once clear of the Edinburgh there was more sea room and heading towards the Shivering Sands towers seven miles distant, time to reflect upon the wisdom of proceeding into the confines of the narrowing channels.

By 0300 Shivering Sands was passed and another relic of the 2nd World War, Red Sand towers stood sentinel on the port bow. TNS came on the air trying to raise the deep drafted *British Tamar* bound for the oil refineries on the north side of the river. With the tanker out of range Peter obliged by relaying the message from the berthing pilot at Coryton.

'No, it will not be possible to berth, wind now 60 knots'.

Lloyd-Jones made up his mind. He still had sufficient sea room before entering the narrow Sea Reach channel. Time enough to make a turn before the full force of the storm arrived. But even as *Stefan Batory* turned, the hurricane hit the Thames estuary from the SSW with wind speeds in excess of force 12

Hurricane 16th October 1987 *Stefan Batory* dragging anchors between the Oaze and Mouse banks

transforming the heaving waves into white spume. The ship listed heavily to port as she clawed her way through the screaming night. Visibility was now zero, and all radar echoes obliterated except the towers. The ship was becoming unmanageable. Lloyd-Jones considered his options. Hove to in the open sea was the obvious choice, if he could get there. There were two of the four channels deep enough - back through the Edinburgh or NE out through the Black Deep. Both would require precise navigation between narrow sand banks, and with no echoes from the buoys, high risk existed. Another consideration was the draft that had increased to nine meters due to the heavy list. The alternative would be to anchor and try to maintain position with the aid of engines.

At first it was impossible for the anchor party to reach the fo'c'sle head. They inched their way, hand over hand along the deck rails, heads down, bodies braced against the force of the storm. The ship approached the Knob anchorage, but no amount of engine or helm movements could turn her. So with the storm astern the starboard anchor was let go, first with six shackles of cable, then four more. With 900 feet of chain stretched taught on the starboard quarter, *Stefan Batory* gradually swung to the SE whereupon the port anchor was let go with six shackles. It was 0445 and she lay there, shaking, with the storm on the beam. But not for long. Within minutes she was on the move again, both anchors dragging. It would only be a matter of time before the ship was hard and fast aground. Despite full sea speed revolutions and full rudder, the ship still would not turn. There was nothing for it, they would need tugs and the sooner the better if they could reach them. TNS replied that tugs were already on their way to vessels grounded in the Southend anchorage, and that two would be diverted to *Stefan Batory*.

Meanwhile the ship dragged through the narrow gap between the Oaze and Mouse shoals. At 0600 the engine-room reported grounding, but the ship continued driving through shoal water towards a wreck marked at only 1.2 meters below the surface. Contact with that could well inflict severe damage, perhaps worse. Both Captain and pilot agreed to the last resort. Sustained maximum revolutions on both engines, hard astarboard, disregarding the anchors. *Stefan Batory* turned slowly, shuddering as mighty waves struck her starboard side, sending spume cascading over her heeling decks. Gradually she gained momentum, the heavy links of the anchor chain lifting from the sea, bar tight until the windlass could bear the strain no longer. The chain parted with a sound like a cannon shot, but at last the vessel was turned and heading away from the boiling shallows towards the deep water of the Warps, and into the wind. At about that time the port anchor was lost also, but these were minor details now that the ship was off the lee shore and hove to with the wind ahead. At last she was under control, although the occasional violent sheer required full speed and rudder correction.

At 0700 the large Alexander tugs *Formidable* and *Sun Anglia* arrived on the scene, with the latter making fast forward helping to hold the ship into the wind. By 0915 conditions had moderated sufficiently to continue passage to Tilbury.

At 1200, all secured at Tilbury stage, Peter Lloyd-Jones walked down the gangway. Some disgruntled passengers asked him why they were late. It had been quite a night!

Chapter Nineteen

Jeddah Interlude

During a spell of leave, by way of a busman's holiday, there came an opportunity to take a temporary post as a relief pilot in the Saudi Arabian port of Jeddah. After only a week as observers, Herbie Jones (Thames North Channel) and I were thrown in at the deep end and told to get on with it. It was customary for the resident Arab pilots to take first pick of the ships, leaving the 'temps' to handle the awkward deep draft cement ships, tankers or large container vessels. The port was very busy with all forty-two berths in action and the 'turn round' averaging only twenty-four hours.

Entry to the port is by means of as narrow channel cut into the coral, through the Outer and Inner Gates, the manoeuvring of large vessels being greatly facilitated by the modern tractor tugs and their excellent Filipino skippers. Made fast fore and aft, their simple 'push/pull' method proved very effective in tandem with the fore and aft movements of the ship's main engine.

Being the port of entry for Mecca, millions of pilgrims arrive from far and wide as every Muslim is expected to make the pilgrimage at least once in a lifetime. With so many mouths to feed there is the daily arrival of a livestock ship and my first job was an old Cunarder, her spacious decks now converted into pens for the carriage of sheep from Australia. With 20,000 of them onboard it was hardly surprising that many died on passage. Of those that perished during unloading, their carcases were strung up over the ship's rails to be cut adrift once the vessel was clear of port limits. The once proud ship made a distressing sight on her departure, the dead sheep mingling with the ghosts of passengers thronging the decks as they waved farewell to Southampton.

Jeddah boatyard - where I was not made very welcome

My next ship was a small coaster inward bound. In the pitch dark I climbed up the ladder from the pilot boat, over the rail, and into a herd of camels crowded on the open deck. I fought my way up to the bridge, gave the Somali captain a piece of my mind, (nobody at the ladder, no lighting) and set course towards the Outer Gate beacons - or so I thought. In fact I couldn't distinguish the beacons from the multi-coloured lights of the port beyond. Luckily we were obliged to stop for a departing ship, time enough to get my bearings.

Jeddah was not the most pleasant port of call. There was hardly time enough for a visiting seaman to go ashore even if he wanted to, and then only with a strict security pass. With temperatures well in excess of 100 degrees it was far preferable to remain onboard in air-conditioned comfort. Much to the annoyance of the engineers, the port authorities required all ships to have main engines on one hour's notice, and many a shift took place in the small hours to squeeze in another vessel.

For the relief pilot however, it was all an exciting adventure. We were issued with a blue uniform, a car and a flat in Amaska village fifteen miles from town, which was luxuriously appointed with a large swimming pool, floodlit tennis and air-conditioned squash courts. Alcohol was of course strictly forbidden, though it was surprising what could be done with a spoonful of yeast mixed into a demi-john of fruit juice! Driving was far more hair-raising than the pilotage! There was one speed, flat out. At traffic lights it was not unlike the Formula One starting grid, with the accelerator pressed to the floor to prevent a shunt from behind.

But it was the reef that provided the most enjoyment. It follows the edge of the beach only a few yards out, and equipped with snorkel and flippers, we would float motionless watching a thousand multi-coloured fish as they swam amongst the coral only inches away. A few lazy strokes and the coral would dip abruptly away into a deep blue bottomless void with the dark shadows of sharks far below.

Friends of mine on the beach near Jeddah. The reef was only yards away

Visits to supermarkets could be a risky business, for with one's trolley half filled, the call to prayer might ring out over the loudspeakers. Everyone was obliged to leave immediately and the store closed for twenty minutes. On the other hand, local shopping for bare essentials was easy. Every garage sold spit roast chickens, melons and the bottled water which was more expensive than the petrol!

I did on occasion fall foul of authority. Having set up my easel in a boat yard, I began painting a fishing boat under construction. Two armed guards approached and having watched unsmiling for a few minutes, abruptly ordered me to leave. They would brook no argument, and with raised voices pointed the way out. Apparently my line of sight included the distant naval dockyard. I could have been a foreign agent and they were taking no chances. Then at the airport on my departure, the x-ray machine detected a set of metal tubes in my baggage. Security guards frog-marched me away for a thorough going over. Nor were they convinced that they were looking at oil paints until I squeezed an inch of black on to each of their palms! I was glad to get home....

Chapter Twenty

Retirement

Soon after becoming a pilot, I had bought myself a sketch book and whilst awaiting a ship at Folkestone, sat on a bollard and drew the harbour scene in front of me. I was so disappointed with the result that I lost interest and two years were to pass before I turned the page. Then came a stroke of luck when I attended my first painting holiday under the tuition of the well-known Sussex artist, Norman Battershill. He proposed that we should express ourselves freely and thereupon demonstrated what he meant. Setting up an easel and large canvas out on the terrace overlooking the spacious grounds, he worked at lightning speed and produced a beautiful 'rough copy' in half an hour, explaining step by step as he progressed. I could hardly believe my eyes. Having been used to spending many hours over a muddy little picture I obviously had a lot to learn.

Added spice to that week was the presence of a film crew that was recording the students' reaction to the new acrylic paint by Windsor & Newton. Their cameras were never far away as we attempted to translate the countryside onto canvas. The rapid drying properties of acrylic, together with Norman's enthusiasm, completely changed my outlook. From that moment, whatever the medium, I determined to work faster and to leave that single brush stroke which by chance had left a pleasing effect, rather than ruin it with a dozen fussy strokes. I returned to my sketch-book with renewed vigor, turned that page and never looked back. From the bridge of a ship there is a ready made seascape in every direction, and on occasions I had to remind myself of the job in hand when passing a Thames barge under full sail or a coaster struggling in heavy weather.

Consequently the sketches are brief impressions rather than detailed drawings, and as the memory dims they provide a constant reminder of those pleasant days on the river. And those tiring long nights!

Cornerways Gallery

Full of enthusiasm, I opened 'Cornerways' gallery in Broadstairs. It was an unusual wedge-shaped property on a corner that provided an outlet for my paintings and those of other local artists, notably Matthew Alexander, whose work in the early 1980s sold for modest hundreds, but which now commands prices of thousands in smart London galleries. He is another great influence and we have enjoyed many a painting holiday together. Visits to Arundel, Bosham, Pinn Mill on the river Orwell, the Dordogne, and the Channel Islands in a small sailing boat, to name but a few. The speed at which Matt works is phenomenal and a large three foot canvas is always completed within three hours!

After only week of opening 'Cornerways' I had a stroke of luck. The producer of a BBC television series had a look round the gallery, bought 10 paintings and asked if I had any 'seconds' available. He bought twenty of these and then tempered my spiraling ego by admitting that the series, to be shot in Ramsgate and Herne Bay, and called *Cocklesea*, was about a failed artist! I have to say that the 6 part series was a failure too!

The gallery is long gone now, and well into retirement we live on the coast of Dorset. We take the occasional busman's holiday on the water, though whenever onboard ship I itch to be up there on the bridge offering my redundant services!

Far off places like the Great Barrier Reef hold a special attraction for me and I jumped at the chance recently when the disembarking pilot invited me ashore for lunch at one of the world's remotest pilot stations - Thursday Island.

Thursday Island from Fort Victoria looking northwest.
The fort was built in 1891 to prevent possible attack on the island's coaling station from various potential enemies

such as France, Russia, America or Japan

Set among a cluster of islands north off Cape York, Thursday Island proved an ideal choice for a European settlement as the fierce natives avoided it, believing the island to be haunted as well as devoid of water. During WWII the island escaped Japanese air attack on account of the graves of Japanese pearl fishermen buried there, even though Darwin and Townsville were bombed at far greater range. This small, hilly island has less than 5,000 inhabitants, the majority of which are the Torres Straits islanders. Its most famous resident was Somerset Maugham who wrote several books here.

The Pilot Station, set back a couple of roads from the jetty, is a large rambling bungalow with accommodation for 10, large lounge, full size snooker room, chartroom, manager's office (run by the coxswain), laundry room and a spacious kitchen presided over by Susan, the full-time cook and bottle-washer. In this part of the world the rainy season is coming to an end in March, but the occasional 'light shower' made conversation impossible under the corrugated iron roof. The fans work overtime, and there is little to do apart from improving upon your best break! To perspire freely, even when sitting still, was quite unavoidable.

Over lunch, my host Wallace Cray told me more about the job, 50 ships a year with the licence covering 2000 miles and the longest pilotage in the world. Whilst on duty they have a roster system similar to Folkestone, usually 3 weeks on followed by a week or two off, depending on traffic. Draft limitation is 40 feet which in some areas gives only 3 foot clearance from an unforgiving bottom! The tides are very strong, with a range of 3 metres. What with 'squat' and other considerations, I rather imagine the Thames to be the safer option! Needless to say, I made full use of my sketchbook on Thursday Island and wondered, had I ever been a Barrier Reef pilot, just how long it would have been before I missed the next transit as I concentrated upon my little watercolour!

When the Torres Strait sea route became a reality for commercial shipping in the early 1800s, navigable passages through the Great Barrier Reef had already been discovered by some of history's most famous naval explorers - Torres (1606), Cook (1770 *Endeavour*), Bligh (1789 Lifeboat), Flinders (1803), Jeffries (1815 *Kangaroo*). The way was now clear for a short cut for ships from Sydney bound China, Java and India.

The first pilotage act took place in 1872, and Thursday Island pilot station became established five years later. Despite the great distances involved and the degree of difficulty, the Barrier Reef pilots enjoy an enviable safety record. The one tragedy occurred in 1890 when the British India's *Quetta* 3300 gross tons was on passage from Brisbane with pilot Eldred Hardinge (ex-Worcester cadet) on the bridge. At 9.14 on a clear moonlit evening, passing between Cape York and Mount Adolphus Island, the ship's bottom was sliced open by an uncharted pinnacle of rock. Mortally wounded with a gaping rent 175 feet long, the ship's momentum cleared the rock, and she sank in 3 minutes with the loss of 134 lives. ¢

* * *

Some of the most stunning scenery in the world is to found in the Norwegian fjords and beyond to Spitzbergen. Onboard Olsen's *Black Watch* as Art Lecturer, I looked forward to what proved to be an unforgettable voyage to the Land of the Midnight Sun, and to within 600 miles of the North Pole.

As we cleared the Western entrance, and set course for the South Goodwin Lightship, I recalled the numerous occasions as a Cinque Ports pilot en route to and from the busiest port in the world. And the many

¢ *The Quetta, Queensland's worst disaster* by John C H Foley, Nairana publications

hours spent on 'Dover Lookout' awaiting orders of ships' arrivals and departures, or better still, an order from an agent whose ship was in port on the other side of the Channel, in Antwerp perhaps, and requiring a pilot for London, post haste. This was always a voluntary job, but it was not often that the pilot 'on turn' refused the bonus that was on offer!

Sognefjord

Balestrand was the first port of call in the magnificent Sognefjord. It is the longest of Norway's fjords at 127 miles, with depths of 4000 feet in places and mountains towering as high above. Then Alesund before continuing our voyage northward crossing into the Arctic Circle and into the narrowing Vestfjord channel between the Lofoten Islands and the mainland. Following the coastal steamer route left little room for error for a vessel of 28,000 tons and seven meter draft. The sensational scenery was made so much more enjoyable by the glorious sunshine, when so often this coastline is covered in thick low cloud and fog. Then tortuous Tjeldsund, Solbergfjord and the ever narrowing channels before passing beneath Sadness Bridge on the approach to Tromso.

Next stop was the small fishing port of Honningsvag where a 40 minute coach trip across a bleak landscape dotted with reindeer, takes you to the sheer cliffs of North Cape, which although at latitude 71 degrees 10 minutes is not quite the most northern part of the Norwegian mainland. At our backs Norway stretched 1,100 miles to the south, whilst ahead lay Spitzbergen, 500 miles distant.

Then north again to Bear Island of Hammond Innes fame, with the sheer granite cliffs shrouded in low cloud. Trawlers in the distance were reaping a bountiful harvest. Cod deep down, and on the surface shoals of fish broke surface as they chased small fry. Ornithologists onboard were in their element with seabirds of all types to be identified. Between the rocky coastline we glimpsed the occasional inlet, home to abandoned whaling stations and refuges for the fishermen.

And so, on to the island of Spitzbergen in the Svalbard (The Cold Lands). To Longyearbyen, and Barentsburg, a small mining outpost leased to Russia. Manned by 750 Ukrainians on a 2 year contract, all are required to work, the men down the coal mines, the women in the cafeterias and the two small factories manufacturing articles from seal or reindeer skin. Their journey to work from the Ukraine is a long one. Two days by train to Murmansk, followed by the 3 day voyage by ship. Under difficult conditions (25 men died in a mine fire in 1996), 350,000 tons of coal is produced each year, and exported by large bulk carriers through the ice-free months, May to November. Our first impressions as we moored alongside a small wooden jetty was of the nearby mine head belching forth thick black smoke from a thin chimney, standing stark against the beautiful backdrop of snow capped mountains and glaciers.

The coal mine at Barentsburg

A concert had been arranged ashore, though the 250 dilapidated wooden steps leading up from the jetty to the small township proved quite a hazard for many passengers. With little else to do through the long dark winter months, music plays an important part. The Ukrainians were delighted to greet such a large audience and their performance was inspired with the music and dance from Russia. They received a standing ovation from the 400 passengers lucky enough to see it.

Black Watch in breathtaking Magdalenafjord, Spitzbergen

Moffen island was to be our most northerly latitude at 80 degrees 02 minutes, and we stopped to see the colonies of walruses as they slept, cavorted and fished to satisfy their insatiable appetites. A wonderful sight, but lovely Magdalena Fjord, where huge glaciers, snow capped mountains, icebergs and even polar bears held us breathless. A lifeboat was lowered for the ship's photographer to get close ups of a family of three bears that had come to the water's edge. The boat returned with enough ice to mix into our glasses of old whisky. It felt like a Christmas morning as we huddled together toasting the unforgettable scene. The ship edged closer to the largest glacier until it seemed within touching distance. One could distinctly hear the cracking ice above us, echoed by the identical sounds from within our glasses. Quite uncanny.

Our return journey brought us through narrowing fjords to Norway's priceless gem. . There didn't seem enough room to turn hard a port into Geirangerfjord, but then, after another S bend, there was little Geiranger nestling at the head of the fjord dwarfed by the majesty of the mountains above. With hardly room to turn, the ship anchored and once again the lifeboats were pressed into service for the short trip ashore, and once again we gazed in awe at the incredible scenery about us. Norway has a population of only 4 million, yet it is hard to believe that only 4% of the country is cultivated. With its endless supplies of North Sea oil and a large modern merchant fleet it has become one of the richest countries in the world. The forestry and fishing industries flourish, and hydro-electricity provides cheap power to the manufacturing industries. Bergen was the last port of call, but after our experiences it appeared rather ordinary, although via the cable car the view is stunning from the top of Mt. Floyen, the fish market is very colourful, and a visit to Edvard Grieg's home is not to be missed.

On our return to Dover, I noticed many changes at the port where I had begun my career in 1967. To have been a Cinque Ports pilot had been very fulfilling, but now in retirement, there are not enough hours in the day!